OBSERVATIONS,
QUESTIONS,
and a few
ANSWERS

By
Mike Turnbull

PREFACE

I would first like to point out that I still don't know the difference between a "Preface" and a "Foreword," so I am going to call this a "Preface" because I am relatively sure I am spelling it correctly. So let's get caught up.

Some of you have read my previous books. Maybe because you bought one or you found a free one in the Hibbing, Ely, or Iowa Lakes Community College Library. Others just waited until I gave you one. Anyway, I am grateful to anyone who has taken the time to read any of my books.

For those who are not familiar with my other books, they have been published in the following order: Random Thoughts of a Stupid Man, More Random Thoughts of a Stupid Man, A Guide to Middle School & Beyond, Semi-Retired and Still Stupid, I Still Own a Flip Phone & Wear Skinny Jeans [Not my best work], Five Days Without iPads, & most recently Retirement Sucks. The middle school and iPad books are intended for younger readers. The other books were written to inspire other "Stupid" men like myself and help those who are trying to guide and mold those "Stupid" men.

Nadine Marsnik, my college freshmen composition teacher, advised me to write about things I know and not stray from that. I have tried to stay true to my heart and stick with her advice. Thus, the "Stupid Man" theme permeates a lot of my writing.

My writing method is still the same. I keep notes all

the time, as Sam Zorman would say, "I enter them in to my hard drive." Sam has a little black book. I write my notes on anything available at the time a thought comes to mind or sometimes whenever the thought resurfaces. I stash the notes, and when I become inspired to write I transfer the notes to a composition notebook. When I get around to it, I type the notes into my computer when I get the urge. Eventually the process culminates in a book. It is my way of updating my status.

I have always enjoyed writing in any capacity. I find it therapeutic. Putting thought to paper allows me to sleep better. Otherwise, I find myself awake at night contemplating the days' events and what's on the agenda tomorrow. It either causes me to lose sleep or creates some bizarre dreams which just baffle me. For example, the other day I saw a sign in a café that said, "STRESSED is just DESSERTS spelled backwards." I couldn't help but wonder, in my 61 years on this planet, why I have I never seen that on a sign or a t-shirt? Thanks for letting me share that; I already feel better.

"Observations, Questions, and a Few Answers" will be my 8th attempt at writing a book. I say "Attempt" because I definitely haven't mastered writing; very few people do. It is a passion of mine, though, and I am thankful that Jansina at Rivershore books is nice enough to continue publishing my attempts. I am truly blessed. To quote Larry Mischke again, "God takes care of stupid people."

I hope you enjoy the read if nothing else. If you do, please recommend it to others. If not, I have been told that my books make for a quick read in the outhouse. Either way, I appreciate the support.

~ Mike Turnbull January 25, 2020 ~

DEDICATION

To my newest grandson Hollis Kent Turnbull. I hope you eventually realize you have been born into a long line of "Stupid Men." Don't blame your father or either one of your grandpas, just pick up the torch, cherish it, and carry it forward proudly. I know you will grow to make us all proud.

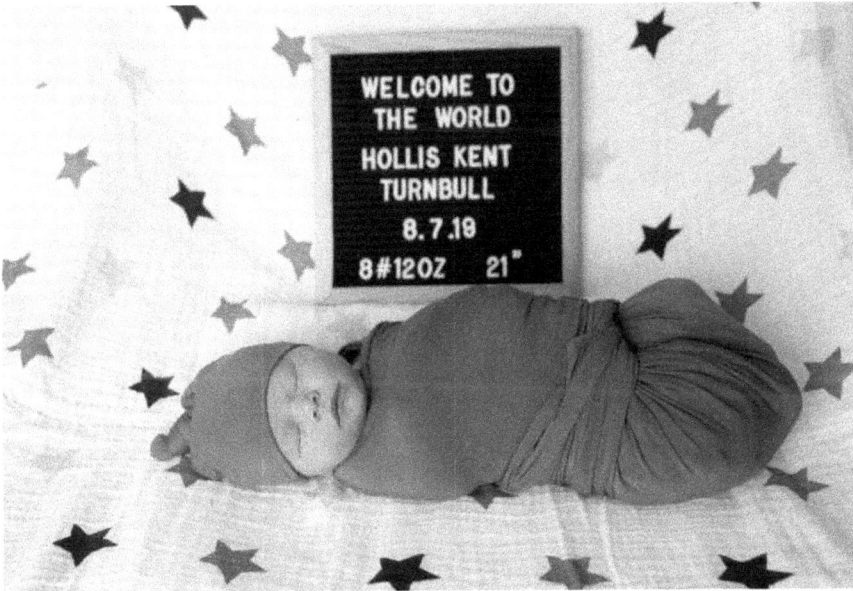

Photo by Alex Turnbull

SPECIAL THANK YOUS

First of all, thank you to my wife Pam. Thanks for being supportive of me in this new adventure in our lives. I know that I was not very good at retirement the past two years, and I am thankful you allowed me to take this new job at Iowa Lakes Community College in Estherville, IA and have been so supportive in making it work. I love you and cherish every moment we manage to spend together these days.

Also thank you to all the people of Iowa Lakes CC and the Estherville that make me feel so welcomed and supported here. I can't tell you how happy and fulfilled I am to be coaching and working fulltime again. Thanks to my first of many Laker Volleyball teams. This first season was a memorable one and I look forward to building on what we started together. Happy Trails to you!

Photo by Mike Turnbull

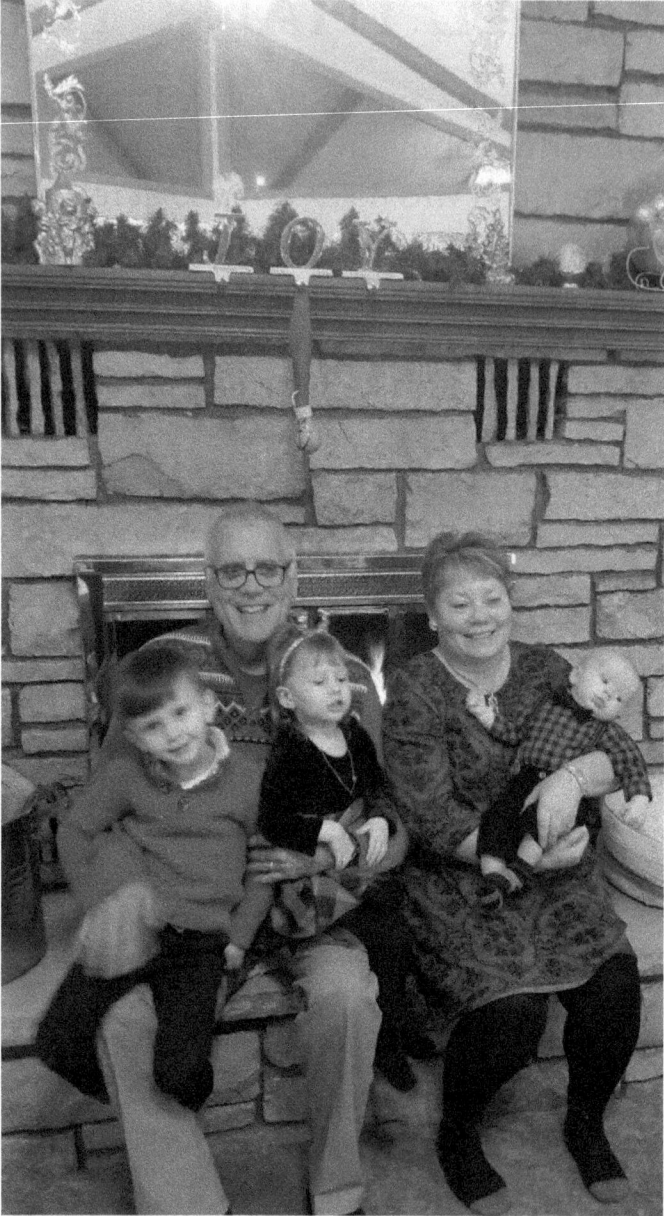

Photo by Alex Turnbull
Mike & Pam with grandchildren Beckett, Brexley & Hollis
Christmas 2019

Photo by Mike Turnbull 2019 Iowa Lakes Volleyball Team L-R: Sydney Swanson, Jada Barker, Lindsey Jensen, Faith Marroquin, Mary Kelly, Evonne Tomlin, Ariel Bozonie, Quiana Coria-Lopez, & Haileigh Smith.

OBSERVATIONS, QUESTIONS, AND A FEW ANSWERS

I went to see the Mr. Rogers movie starring Tom Hanks. Great movie, amazing story, life impacting! Tom Hanks was fabulous. I left the theatre with this thought: If Fred Rogers was doing his show today, I am sure he would wear Skechers slip-ons instead of those lace-up sneakers. I love my Skechers and I am not a big fan of lace-ups anymore. Age or wisdom?

President Trump is stressing me out. Up until now, I have managed to ignore most of his antics. Now he has taken me back to 1979. I have never been able to keep them straight. Iran or Iraq? Baghdad and Beirut, which country are they in? Is it Koran or Quran? I was okay with our last President. Obama + Osama Bin Laden + Al-Qaeda = Afghanistan.

I maintain two birdfeeders outside my apartment window in Estherville, IA. I have noticed that Iowa squirrels are the same as Minnesota squirrels, in that they both think they are birds. Fear not, I will continue my battle against squirrels; now the battle just takes place on two fronts. All for the good of the cause.

Photo by Mike Turnbull [I have always appreciated a good battle with squirrels.]

What plumber fixed the frozen pipes at the Evergreen Restaurant at the Grand Ely Lodge [GEL] last year? They froze again this year; definitely not good advertising.

I have developed a guilt complex. I have seen the

flooding in Nebraska and Iowa, and I have come to realize it has a lot to do with snow levels in Minnesota. If I am right, 2020 doesn't look good for the farmers down here. I was at home over Christmas break enjoying beautiful winter setting in Ely. There is a lot of snow up there. I hope the wonderful people here in Estherville don't hate on me too much this spring.

Speaking of guilt complexes:

To: Fellow Minnesota Vikings fans,

I apologize in case it was my fault. I have two Vikings jerseys, both given to me by my son. They are both throw-backs. The white one is "PAGE" #88 and the purple one is "FOREMAN" #44. The "PAGE" jersey was undefeated and "FOREMAN" was sitting at .500 going into today. I wear them when I watch the Vikes. My usual viewing venue of choice is the Winton Roadhouse but this year most of my Vikings' game days have been spent at Woody's Pizza in Estherville. Anyway, after much personal debate, I went with the "FOREMAN" jersey for the play-off game versus the 49ers. Obviously, bad choice on my part.

There is a Bi-Product plant south of Estherville. Are bi-products the same thing that is in sausage and cannibal meat at Zups' Grocery in Ely?

It has been interesting being in Iowa for all the pre-caucus hype. A little overwhelming, though. I really can't believe all the time and money all the democratic presidential hopefuls are spending here in Iowa. I'm sure this is old hat for anyone who has grown up in

Iowa, but I have found it intriguing. The only conclusions that I have come to so far are, Tom Steyer cannot go head to head with Donald Trump and win. Also, I really don't believe President Trump fears Elizabeth Warren.

Baseball teams at all levels have been stealing signs forever. All of a sudden MLB is all over the Astros and Red Sox for stealing signs and considering how to punish them. Is it because they went high tech to steal signs? If that is truly the issue, then why all the talk about implementing electronic strike zones? You can't have it both ways!

There are trees in Iowa. Strange looking, to say the least. They have huge trunks, only three branches, no leaves or needles, and no fruit. Sometimes the branches just sit there and other times I have seen them spinning in circles. They are impossible to climb. I have seen them come by on flatbed trailers after they have been logged. They are so big that the trunks are usually cut up and transported on at least three or four trucks. The branches are always transported separately. Not going to lie, I am partial to the white pines, birch and popples in Ely.

Photo by Mike Turnbull

I know I have asked this before, but I still have not received a valid answer. Is there such a thing as left handed underwear? This is probably too much information for some of you, but when I stand at a urinal, I use my right hand to open my underwear and left hand to pee. Anyway, after Christmas I bought some new briefs. I am having difficulty opening them to pee, they open to the left. I hope this is just a wardrobe malfunction because I like my Fruit of the Loom briefs. Despite my appreciation for Michael Jordan, I would hate to have to go back to Hanes underwear.

Traveling east on Highway 20 in Iowa today. Passed a sign that read, "Ditch # 206." Did the Iowa Department of Transportation count all the ditches in Iowa, and if so, why aren't they all numbered?

Photo by Mike Turnbull

I have been working at my new job at Iowa Lakes Community College in Estherville, IA for about six months now. It has been a great experience. I love the work environment. I feel welcomed, supported, and appreciated every day. Compared to other schools and colleges I have worked at throughout my career, Iowa Lakes appears to have a female employee majority and all but one of my supervisors is a woman, including the President and Dean of Students. Maybe there is something to be said for women running the show. [Side note: Nikki Haley, if you read this book, please consider a Presidential run in 2024! P.S. I am enjoying reading your book right now.] No job is perfect, but this place is a great place to work and I am glad they had the faith to hire me. I do wish it was closer to home, but having a second home when you are 60 years old is pretty cool. "LAKER PROUD"

I got a little excited today. I heard Jennifer Wojcicki doing the weather report on the local radio station in Estherville. Felt like I was back in Ely. I sat in my truck and said "Jennifer Vuuuu CheeeetSkiiiiii!" Come on, you know what I am talking about. Repeat after me "Jennifer VuuuuCheeetSkiiii!" You know that brightens your day!

I am getting real tired of trying to prove to re-Capatcha that I am not a robot that has taken over my computer when I attempt to copy & paste attachments. [Side note: to all my ex-players and students: Yes, I said copy & paste and believe it or not, I now know how to do it. Credit goes to Sarah, Molly, and Sandy.] Back to re-Captcha before I lose my train of thought. Even though I can find traffic lights, fire hydrants, motor cycles, bridges, palm trees, crosswalks, etc. with the best of them, I am not a robot so please give me a break. I do apologize for not always reading your instructions and pushing "Verify" too soon. One question though, what is the logic behind throwing in the pictures where you click on "Skip"?

I am definitely not a food critic, but I am going to tell you that there is no comparison between the chicken wings at the Winton Roadhouse and the wings at Woody's in Estherville. Rich Hrkas, you win hands down! Please re-open the Roadhouse this summer; I will be home in May. I want to add something here: West O Smoked Red Beer wins over Castle Danger George Hunter and the menu at Woody's is way better than the Roadhouse.

I feel blessed to have two church homes in my life. The Ely Methodist Church will always be my home church but the Estherville Methodist Church has become my home church away from home. Thanks to Pastor Craig Haberman in Ely and Pastor Kevin Moore in Estherville for being such outstanding preachers and people. Both of you do outstanding work. I also want both church communities to know that you are doing things very well. A person can't help walking into either church and not feel welcomed and supported.

I am in the middle of my first winter in Northwestern Iowa. I'll take northern Minnesota winter weather anytime. I am a big fan of watching local newscasts and listening to the Killer Bee 95.9. I have decided that in the winter you don't need to pay much attention to the temperature; it is all about wind chill factor. Winter is not my favorite time of the year anyway and now 40 to 50 MPH wind gusts and freezing rain? Yuck! I am kind of excited, though; tonight's forecast on Sioux Land News said to expect freezing fog in the morning. I had no idea fog could freeze, so I'm looking forward to seeing that. The upside to all this? I am betting that spring comes to Estherville weeks before it does in Ely, so only 1 ½ more months of winter. Maybe Ground Hogs' Day actually matters here. I am a little disappointed, though. I was told by a local the other day that Emmet County is traditionally the coldest, snowiest, and windiest county in Iowa. Nobody mentioned that in my interview in August, and I have never seen that in any Chamber brochures. Whatever happened to full disclosure?

Photo by Mike Turnbull: Freezing fog or freezing rain and wind? Still, yuck!

I don't know what this has to do with anything. I watched the Grammy Awards show for a while tonight. I don't claim to be a Rap fan, but I do like old school Rap and I have admitted in the past to being a closet Nelly fan. Actually, I have admitted it more than once, so I guess I am officially out of the closet. I have also had my moments listening to Tupac. Anyway, to cut to the chase, how cool was it to see Steven Tyler/ Aerosmith and Run DMC perform "Walk This Way" on the Grammy's? I really enjoyed the camera panning around to everyone rocking out, including Smokey Robinson, Flavor Flav, and Lizzo. I never thought a Rap song would qualify for classic status, but "Walk This Way" may have pulled it off.

I want to point something out. In my other books I have either dated or numbered my random thoughts. I want you to know that in this book there is no logical order. Kind of like my life. I have been taking notes for about six months so far. Every once in a while, I pull them out and add them to the book. Sometimes when I am typing, other thoughts come to mind and I add those in. You get additional time to think when you type with one or two fingers. When I am really on a roll, I utilize a third finger or my left hand gets involved. My point here is that I am older now and chronological or logical order sometimes fails me. So, if you have been trying to figure a timeline into this book, stop; it really doesn't exist. These are truly just random observations, questions, and a few answers.

I want to clear up a rumor. I do not live in a nursing home when I am in Estherville. Truth be told, I do live in an apartment on the Good Samaritan Campus. I rent an apartment in the Friendship Terrace, which is designated as senior independent living. There are two other buildings on the campus: one is assisted living and the other is a nursing home. Pretty convenient, but I am hoping that when I become a candidate for the other two buildings, I will not be working at Iowa Lakes CC and I will be back home in Ely with my wife fulltime. It will be up to her where she wants to put me.

After the Christmas holiday I bought a membership to the Regional Wellness Center in Estherville. It had nothing to do with a new year's resolution. I just wanted to get back to lap swimming. I haven't done that since we lived in Hibbing. I am really enjoying the swimming and I have also started weightlifting and doing some cardio work again. Today I took another step: I went to adult water polo to check it out. Loved it! Celebrated by going to Woody's and having two beers and a sausage sandwich. I will be going back to water polo. One hour straight up in the deep end of the pool; great workout! I am now considering buying a key fob so I can access the RWC 24/7. I'm hooked. I hope the people of Estherville and the surrounding area appreciate the RWC. It is an outstanding facility and service. Ely is considering some form of a recreation center. If the people in Ely could see the RWC, they would pass a bond with no doubts. I just hope that when Ely makes a decision, I am there to vote and a pool is in the plans.

I am looking forward to the Super Bowl next week. I would be okay with either team winning. Because of my current location, I guess I should lean toward the Chiefs. This is the first time in my life that I have lived in a state that has no professional teams. Seems like you can root for anyone you want. As far as football goes, I have noticed more Bears fans in Iowa than anything else. Now as far as college ball goes, that is entirely different beast. You are either a Hawkeye fan or a Cyclone fan. I have come across UNI fans every once in a while. The UNI fans tend to be very subtle about it. It is a lot more obvious with the Iowa and Iowa Ste fans. I realize Drake is in the mix but apparently, I don't travel in those circles. I have noticed that they all unite when I wear any Minnesota Gopher apparel. I am definitely one up on all of them this year as far as football goes. I know the Hawkeyes got Floyd of Rosedale but consider the overall season. "Row the Boat"!

"The connections we make in a course of a life. Maybe that is what heaven is."

~ Fred Rogers ~

*Photo by Mike Turnbull: Painted mural in Westport, MO
Night before AFC title game.*

Photo by Mike Turnbull: I don't know how Chiefs fans did this.

I have seen it on shirts and hats. I saw a banner the other day [Side note: I know what yesterday, today, and tomorrow are. Is the other day one of the other four days of the week?] and I hear about it on the radio and television. I have been over to Spirit Lake and the Lake Okoboji area several times now and haven't been able to find it. Where is the University of Okoboji and why don't they ever show their sports scores on television or in the newspaper?

A few years ago, the popular phrase "My bad!" always irritated me when I heard it from anyone. To me it is used as a way to quickly dismiss an incident and a half- hearted effort at taking responsibility. Don't get me wrong; I am guilty of using the phrase. I would like to think rarely, but I am guilty of dropping a "My bad" here and there. The phrase that is currently used and in the same manner is: "It is what it is." I refuse to cave into using this phrase. To me it is an indicator of lost hope and denial of accountability. I would prefer phrases like, "I'll fix that," "We need to work on that," Let's do something about that," etc. At least there is indications of accountability, hope, and reaching out to others for help. Just saying!

Can you believe postage stamps cost 55 cents? I realize that the price of everything has gone up during my lifetime despite getting smaller or the quality diminishing. At least the postage stamp has improved; you don't even have to lick them anymore.

Do newscasters and sportscasters on television that color their hair realize that HD television doesn't do them any favors? You can still see the gray roots. I have never colored my hair, it wouldn't fool my family, friends, and co-workers and they are the people that matter most to me.

I had dinner at Brit's Pub in Minneapolis Thursday night; great BLT by the way! Enjoyed the house music: Beatles, Elton John, and the Rolling Stones — perfect!

I am definitely jealous of John Bolton. He is getting free advertising for his soon-to-be-released book. In the last few days any reports on the Trump impeachment include a discussion of Bolton's new book. I'm sure he was disappointed when the Senate voted against bringing in witnesses. I think a lot of people were. I have been racking my brain, but I can't think of anything I have witnessed or heard in any room that I have been in that could entice millions of people to buy my book. Hopefully I can make enough money to help with gas driving back and forth between Ely and Estherville. If sales really take off, maybe I can pay for next year's membership at the RWC and a few beers at the Roadhouse and Woody's. I know what you're thinking, "Big dreamer!" Hey, I am a simple man with simple needs [self-proclaimed "Stupid Man"]; a guy can only hope.

They probably don't realize it, but the ladies in my apartment building pass their wisdom on to me daily and I am thankful. I have always paid attention to what people say when I ask them "How are you doing today?" or "What are you up to today?" Yesterday I asked one of the ladies, that I know is over 80, "What are you doing today?" her response was, "Whatever I please, because I can." Today I asked another lady the same question. Her answer was, "I'm moving," I asked, "Where are you moving to?" She laughed, "Not moving out, I am just moving. When you are 90 and you start moving, you just keep moving." She continued to walk briskly down the hall. My all-time favorite response to the question, "How are you doing today?" came from a gentleman at church that I estimated to be in his 80s. He said, 'I am on the right side of the grass. That beats the hell out of great. How are you doing?"

I read a feature article in the Outdoors section of the Minneapolis Star Tribune yesterday. The article was the first in a series written by Mark Neuzil. The article was about Charles Eastman, who passed away 81 years ago. Charles was a Native American author, physician, and lecturer. The series is about nature writers in Minnesota. The article caught my attention because I suspect that Charles is a relative of my deceased dear friend, Dennis Eastman. While reading the article, I came across a quote by Charles that I would like to share. "In civilization there are many deaf ears and blind eyes. In the great laboratory of nature there are endless secrets yet to be discovered."

If you are still reading this book, thank you. It was not my original intent to continue along the "Stupid Man" path. I was contemplating [that is what I call it when I am thinking hard] writing a book with the premise I was sent to Iowa to infiltrate the community and find out what Iowans really think of Minnesotans. I also wanted to find out if any of the Iowa jokes told in Minnesota have any merit. I gave up on both ideas. So far all I can report is that Iowans are just as nice as Minnesotans. Don't get me wrong, both states also have their share of idiots. I am glad that Minnesota laid claim to "Minnesota Nice" but Iowa is right there with us and the sweet corn is better down here. If you continue reading you will notice more comparisons between the two states, and I will continue with "Observations, Questions, and a Few Answers." I am just following Mrs. Marsnik's advice, "Stick to what you know."

I have been traveling a lot lately for volleyball recruiting. When I get the time to sit down for dinner, I usually go to a local pub & eatery and sit at the bar. I don't see much sense in occupying a table when I am by myself. I often take note on my receipt to see how the bartender has identified me. These are some of the latest: "First guy," "Not bald," "Polite," 'Old guy," "Accent," and my favorite, "Married." [I hope my wife is reading this.]

I am really enjoying the morning lap swimming at the RWC in Estherville. I have also been doing some weightlifting and cardio work. I think I am somewhat addicted. This might sound a little weird [try not to judge and if you agree just nod]: when I come into the RWC and punch in my membership number, I enjoy hearing the computer-generated voice that says, "Welcome." Much more pleasant than the voice on a Google search or Google Maps. There is something about a pleasant voice saying "Welcome" at 6:30 AM. Okay, now that I have said it publicly, that is weird, but it is too late to take it back. Please just nod if you are with me either way on this one.

If you haven't heard, this is a census year. I decided to Google a few things to see how I stack up before a census taker stops by to talk to me. Most of these figures are based in 2018. Keep in mind the reported world population was 7.53 billion and U.S. 327.2 million.

Platform	Active Users World	Active Users U.S.	Non-Users world
Facebook	1 billion	220.5 million	6.5 billion
Instagram	800 million	107 million	6.7 billion
Twitter	262 million	68 million	7.24 billion

I am not a social media user. So, every once in awhile I like to check some of these numbers. I am always be asked why I am not on Facebook and being told everyone is on Facebook. Plus, a lot of subjects or places you look up on the internet require you to be on Facebook to access the websites. It is comforting to know I have anywhere from 6.5 to 7.24 billion people that are somehow managing to function without being connected to social media. Who knew?

Iowa is the hub of the news media world tonight, caucuses. On the 5:00 local news tonight they said Iowa ends up predicting the Presidential winner about 50% of the time. On the Democratic side I am hoping that Yang or Klobuchar gets into the top 4 just to shake things up moving forward. It will be interesting to see how Iowans respond to basically being ignored by Michael Bloomberg, compared to the blitz put on by all the other candidates.

Photo by Mike Turnbull [Beckett, Hollis, & Brexley]
Have I mentioned how much I enjoy being Grandpa Mike?

My life in Estherville took a large step forward last

weekend. I found a barber in Spirit Lake about 15 minutes away. There is no barber in Estherville. I am not opposed to going to a salon, but I'll take an old-time barbershop anytime. I found Dave's Barbershop. Pretty excited! Good haircut and a Jeanie neck and shoulder massage after haircut. Bonus, I got to watch John Wayne's "Rio Bravo" on DVD while I was in the chair. Dave gave me the senior discount and the haircut was only $13. Dave is a real nice guy. I hope he stays in business at least until I am done working at Iowa Lakes.

While I am on the topic of personal grooming, it is time for me to get home or my wife to come down here for a few days. I am really missing her and my toenails are missing her. They are out of control and she is the only one that I trust to cut them. I definitely don't trust myself. I don't know if Pam agrees but I feel that distance does make the heart grow fonder.

I think I have figured out this "Freezing Fog" thing. I still think it is all just frost but every time the local weather broadcasters mention "Freezing Fog," this is what I see outside.

Photos by Mike Turnbull

There is an insurance commercial on television that makes a reference to people turning into their parents. I have picked up on one of my mother-in-law's behaviors. I have started taking notes on the church bulletin during Sunday services. She usually writes down names to pray for or a Bible verse she wants to revisit. I take notes during the children's sermon and the main sermon. I am stealing ideas for when I do children's sermons or notes for books. Last week Pastor Moore did a sermon on 10 reasons why people leave the church. I was intrigued because as he was working through the ten reasons, I started relating the concept to other facets of my life. I thought of student retention at the college, people sticking with jobs, teams, relationships, etc. I felt like several of the reasons were applicable to groups and organizations other than just the church. Pastor Moore listed these reasons from 10 to 1. The following were my rough notes. I hope you find something in this that you can relate to.

10. Can't find community

9. Internal drama

8. Unresolved conflict

7. Controlling leaders and unskilled teachers

6. Social cliques and nepotism

5. Copying or following a model other than Jesus

4. Infiltrated by politics

3. Not authentic/false sense of reality

2. Feel lonely

1. Don't find Jesus

Please think it over for yourself. I couldn't help not to think that reasons 2-4 and 6-10 are applicable to why people leave group situations. I think if you replaced "Jesus" with "Guidance, Hope, or Forgiveness" In reason #1 that one applies also. In today's society, we all need to feel and be cognizant of #10 community.

I started watching the State of the Union Address tonight. Tried to be as open minded as possible going in. It felt it would fit right into "Observations, Questions, and a Few Answers," so hang with me. Not, sure but was it only Republicans that stood up and clapped most of the time? Democrats seemed edgy and guarded, a few polite/golf claps. In the past few years, I have lived in or traveled to the Midwest, central plains, southwest, great lakes region, Mississippi Valley, Southeast, and California. I have not seen the economic boon that President Trump referenced. I was very amused by Nancy Pelosi, sitting behind Mr. Trump.

She was either listening to an audio book or there was vodka in that water glass. She appeared very awkward throughout the speech. She definitely didn't hide her reaction to Trump's bullet points, if and when she was listening. She is the main reason I continued watching. SNL and late night talk show hosts are going to eat this whole thing alive. Who were the women in the white outfits? Health care and immigration moments in the speech were made for a pretty testy audience. I have a feeling the Impeachment Hearings are going to be ugly tomorrow. Prescription prices have gone down, my ass! My Enbrel costs $4,200+ every month. Okay, that is it, this is all I can take. I am going back to ESPN. I don't know Rush Limbaugh but I don't think he is the greatest fighter I will ever meet. I would put my mom, mother-in-law, and sister Terri in that category. Presidential Medal of Freedom? That is final; I am changing the channel. Maybe somebody has the final results of the Iowa Caucus. [Nope!] I watched the local news after I was sure the State of the Union Address was over. I hadn't noticed that President Trump and Speaker Pelosi didn't make eye contact and didn't shake hands when Mr. Trump came to the podium. Then to cap it off, Speaker Pelosi tore up President Trump's speech that she had been presented with at the beginning of the night. Are you kidding me? It is embarrassing to think that these are two of the major players in our national government. Grow up and be leaders we can be proud of and want to follow!

Maybe I should change the title of this book to "Observations, Questions, A Few Answers, and an Occasional Rant!"

According to NAPO [National Association of Pizza Operators], there are 3 billion pizzas sold in the United States each year. According to McDonald's statistics, it is estimated they have sold 55 billion burgers since 1994. It is estimated that there will be 223.2 million Facebook users in 2023. There were 68 million Twitter users in the first quarter of 2019. There are 328.23 million people in the U.S. It seems obvious to me that if you want to get a message out there, it would be a lot more efficient to put the message on a pizza box or hamburger wrapper.

"Labeling people based on race, gender, and other characteristics has gotten way out of hand in America today. It is destructive and ironically it is limiting. We are more than the sum of our labels." ~ Nikki Haley ~ from her book "With All Due Respect"

There are several times in any given day that I experience "Captain Obvious" moments or hear phrases uttered by others or myself. When I get in my truck in the morning and start it to let it run for a while because it is 10 below zero, a message appears on my dash that reads, "Caution ice & snow are possible." Duh!

February is Heart Health Awareness month. Dr. Oz did a feature on the Today show. He addressed three categories and used three categories to rank them. This is what I got out of it. Thought I'd share.

DIET

Good	Better	Best
Dark Chocolate	Nuts	Broccoli/ Vegetables

EXERCISE

Good	Better	Best
Stand & walk every 30 minutes	7,500 steps per day	10 Minutes vigorous exercise every day

REDUCING STRESS

Good	Better	Best
Meditate	Family time	Community Service

"The Russians are not our friends and will never be our friends!"

~ Nikki Haley's advice to President Trump when she was serving in the UN ~

Yesterday was "National Clean Out Your Computer Day." How did you do?

February Is Black History Month and I want to make this contribution. To my knowledge and a few Google searches I am confident most of this account is correct. I want to raise up Eddie Meyers. I went to school with Eddie at Pemberton Township H.S. in New Jersey during my freshmen and sophomore year. I mention him, because like I have told a lot of people over the years, Eddie is the best athlete I have ever competed with or against. I say competed with, but I was just one of the boys trying to survive in his man's world. I also remember him being a really nice guy. This is what I know to be true.

Pemberton Township 1977 [Football, Track & Wrestling]

US Naval Academy 1981

Downtown Athletic Club Football Player of the Year

All-American Football, Wrestling & Track

Navy's 4th All-Time Rusher

Served in the Gulf War

5 Pre-Seasons & 1 full season with Atlanta Falcons

Went on to become Regional President for PNC Bank in Atlanta

Daughter Elana won a bronze & silver medal in Olympic Bobsledding

Look him up sometime. His accomplishments are well worth noting.

Photos from www.pnc.com

Sunday night on the Oscar Ceremony Bong Joon-ho, the director of "Parasite" quoted Martin Scorsese in one of his acceptance speeches. He attributed Scorsese for telling him, "The most personal is the most creative." That thought inspired the following observation.

Another thing that I enjoy about lap swimming in the morning, that I actually find liberating, is that I get to wear my Speedos. It is the only time and place I wear them. They keep me from drying out. They are a little tight and not exactly comfortable, but they do prevent the burning sensation I would experience if I wasn't wearing them. Also, I am sure that I would have to deal with discomfort the rest of the day. I apologize to those of you that know me. I am sure you will have a hard time getting the image of me wearing Speedos out of your mind.

Sounds like New Hampshire will be announcing a primary winner on the 10:00 news tonight. A little more efficient than the Iowa Caucus, which still hasn't officially declared a winner on the Democratic side.

Okay, I can't put you through this any longer. Hopefully nobody has been emotionally scarred. I mentioned wearing Speedos when I lap swim in the morning. Apparently, I didn't clarify myself. I wear Speedo goggles. My eyes are sensitive to the chlorine in the pool. The goggles keep my eyes from burning and drying out. They are a little tight and not the most comfortable but they do the job. To ease the minds of those of you who know me, I still wear my baggy old navy-blue swimsuit that I have owned for several years. Don't worry; it is safe to come to the pool at the RWC and Fall Lake in the summer.

Sorry to hear that Andrew Yang is dropping out of the Democratic Presidential campaign. I liked some of his ideas. A Buttitieg-Yang ticket might be interesting. I do think the Democrats might have a better chance to defeat President Trump if they get down to one candidate as soon as possible. They need to unite behind one person and end all the nonsense and division. On a personal note, I am looking for a candidate that will approve mining exploration in the Ely, MN area, not cut Social security or Medicare, and not named Donald Trump. It worries me because I am not sure that person has been put in front of us yet.

Roy Williams [University of North Carolina Men's Basketball Coach] conducted a press conference the other night after a frustrating loss to Notre Dame. I found some solace in listening to a coach that I have respect and admiration for vent about what has been a frustrating winter for the Tarheel Nation. He said something along the lines of, "You have two options: you can either curl up in the fetal position and cry or you can continue to compete!" He went on later to say, "There are no options. You are either all in or you can leave!" I hope his underclassmen got the message because I am pretty sure he means it. I really liked his second statement. In all my years as an athlete and a coach, I have always believed that the fondest seasons I remember were with the teams that were "ALL IN."

Roy and his Tarheels are having a rough year, but I am sure they will bounce back quickly next year. The personnel might change a little though.

Our minister preached on heaven today. Somewhere during the sermon he mentioned reuniting with friends, family, and loved ones that have gone before us. I find this thought a bit stressful. I am starting to believe I have a pretty good shot at getting to heaven, at least 50/50. If I do, I hope either my wife or my mother-in-law are there or everyone has name tags. Unlike my wife or mother-in-law, I am terrible with names. Facial recognition, no problem. Names, not so much. Another thing that concerns me; I am pretty sure I know a few people in hell. If I am lucky enough to go to heaven, I hope there is time for a side trip to hell. I would like to stop by and say hi and check it out. When I am traveling I never pass up a side trip if at all possible to see new places, meet new people, or visit with old acquaintances.

I see that some Little League Associations are dropping the use of "Astros" on hats and jerseys because of the now negative connotation. Leaves me to wonder if Corona Beer will have to go through a rebranding process? I have already noticed that when I watch the Corona Beer commercials on television and they mention "Find your beach," my thoughts turn toward cruise ships and airplanes.

I have always been a casual fan of wrestling. I know just enough to appreciate the sport but I have a long way to go before I understand all the nuances. Probably because I am spending so much time in Iowa, but I have watched more wrestling this winter than I have in my entire life. I have watched on television and live, high school and college. One of my many questions is: Do wrestlers ever get their ears back or is cauliflower ear permanent? So far, I have been thankful for my time in Iowa. I have met a lot of nice people and my knowledge base on pigs, corn, wind turbines, and wrestling is expanding daily. I have tried to share some of this newfound knowledge in Ely, but nobody has shown much interest. Fair play I guess, because I haven't been able to strike up a good conversation pertaining to copper-nickel mining and watersheds with anyone in Iowa.

Sometimes when I am on the computer and I am trying to open a file, the computer gives me the option of opening a new window or new tab. I have no idea what the difference is? I'll save that for sometime when I have absolutely nothing else to do.

Halloween is my 4th favorite holiday, but I do embrace it.

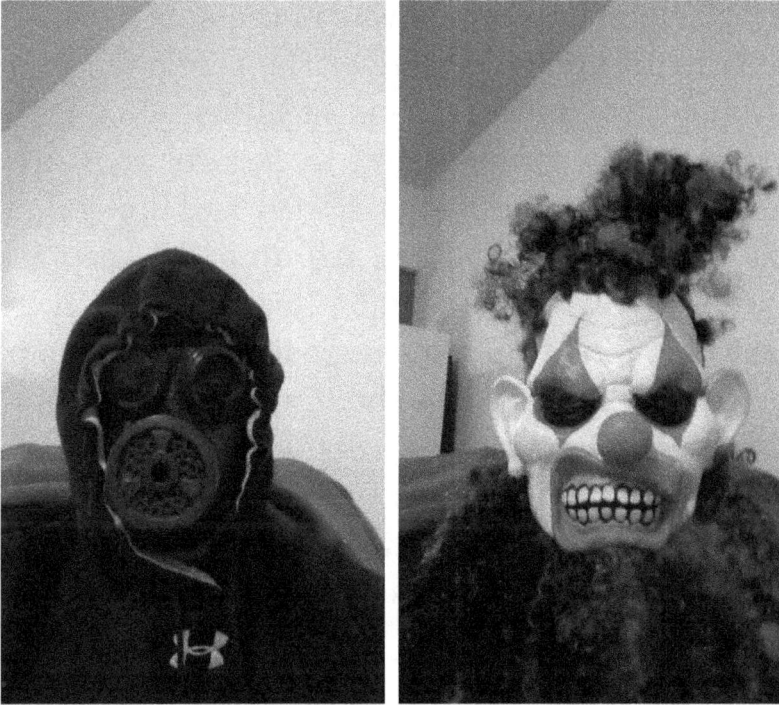

Photos by Mike Turnbull

Don't rush to judgment. Saves a lot on the amount of candy handed out at the front door.

I have avoided this topic for a few weeks now, but I can't take it anymore. I don't think this will make or break book sales, so I am just going to throw a few thoughts out there. Keep in mind the title of my first book is "Random Thoughts of a Stupid Man." I am referring to the death of Kobe Bryant. The fact that I just wrote that bothers me. Several other people died in that helicopter crash, including young kids and relatively young adults. Tragic? Yes. Sad? Yes. Fair? No. I am torn by how I feel about all the attention our media and society have given this unfortunate event. Yesterday's Celebration of Life was impressive but it leaves me with an internal struggle. The sports fan in me is intrigued. My father side is sad because of the losses the victims' families have to endure. My Christian side wants me to be compassionate and non-judgmental. Then the cynical side rises up and I keep asking myself, "Why are we making this about pretty much just Kobe?" In my lifetime there have been wars, plane crashes, bombings, mass shootings, etc. None of these have received the attention that Kobe is getting. I have a vague memory of when President Kennedy was assassinated. I may be wrong but I think the funeral proceedings lasted three days on television. I hope that all the vendors and the NBA find a way to send the profits being made off of #8 and #24 jerseys and "Mamba Life" t-shirts and hats to a worthy cause. I guess that is the root of my internal struggle with this tragic accident and all that surrounds it. What makes anyone or anything worthy? What is a life worth? If this scenario was changed, say Kobe was running for a political office, the media and society would have smeared him out of the campaign by now. Every skeleton in his closet would have been brought to the public forefront. I wouldn't wish that on any human being. Back to the question, what is a life worth? What is your life worth? What is my life worth? Final question, who is worthy of deciding? For now, I will find comfort in the belief that God ultimately will decide and he won't put his decision on Twitter.

Best thing I heard today, actually I read it on someone's t-shirt. "I had my patience tested. The results were negative."

I read in the Ely Echo that Mayor Novak is caught in the middle of a "Tweetstorm" over him suggesting that people boycott Fortune Bay Casino because the Bois Forte tribe has come out in support of a proposed legislative bill that would basically shut down the Twin Metals' proposed mining project in the Ely area. Question, is a "Tweetstorm" or "Twitterstorm" pretty much the same as a "Hissy Fit"?

I don't own a Peleton, pretty sure I can't afford one. I do really like the television commercials. Love the quote, "You didn't wake up to be mediocre today."

I had to buy toilet paper for my apartment on Saturday. My usual brand wasn't available so I bought Northern Quilted. Used it for the first time this morning, I may never go back to my usual, might be a life changer.

First Super Tuesday tomorrow. Leap year was tough on the candidates. That extra day must have allowed more time for soul searching. Amy Klobuchar, Tom Steyer, and Pete Buttigieg all dropped out. I still have a hard time believing that the democrats can bring someone forward to win the Presidential race. It seems that there only way in is if Donald Trump does or says something to take himself out. It seems to me that he does that on a daily basis but it never sticks.

I am starting to think there is no such thing as a political expert anymore. 24 hours before Super Tuesday, political analysts were writing off Joe Biden and tipping the Democratic race toward Bernie. I have not seen all the results this morning, but when I went to bed last night it appeared that Biden was kicking ass and racking up states and delegates. I think that Elizabeth Warren will be the next to drop out. It was a huge message to the rest of us when her home state [Massachusetts] didn't give her the endorsement. We should probably follow suit. I think I will go back to watching ESPN and see where Todd McShay and Mel Kiper have their latest NFL mock draft leader board at. They have just as good a chance of getting it right as the political analysts do. If they all strike out, there is always weather forecasting.

I saw a sign in a public bathroom that read, "Do not flush anything in the toilet other than toilet paper." Made for a miserable bathroom experience; they didn't even provide rubber gloves or tongs.

"What we have here is a failure to communicate." ~Line from the Cool Hand Luke" movie starring Paul Newman~ I have been noticing lately how more and more people don't fully respond to texts and emails. For example, I messaged a volleyball recruit, "What would be a good time to call you tomorrow?" Her response, "Yes."

Pretty sure you can only see this in Estherville, IA. Estherville Lincoln Central H.S. is called the "Midgets." It still humors me when the cheerleaders cheer, "Go Big Red Midgets!"

Photo by Mike Turnbull

Quote from "Quiet Strength," a book by Tony Dungy. "God's plans don't always follow human logic. We often can't see what God is doing in our lives, but God sees the whole picture and his plan for us clearly."

I am feeling like it is fairly late in the process of volleyball recruiting for 2020. We still need to sign a couple more hitters. Is there any other job besides coaching that depends on 18-year-old kids to determine the level of success on the job? I have several volleyball prospects on the hook for the 2020 class and I am waiting semi-patiently for them to make a decision about where they want to attend and play volleyball next year. Lately a popular response from the prospect has been, "I am still weighing my options." What does that mean? If they told me that they were praying on it or discussing it with their parents, I would get that. "Weighing my options," I find a little confusing. These prospective recruits need to understand that it is March and options are starting to run out. Also, how much does an option weigh, anyway?

I had a great weekend. On Saturday morning I swam laps from 7–8:00. Drove up to the cities to see my sister who just got out of the hospital after surgery earlier in the week. I stayed the night with my son's family and got to spend time with my grandchildren. Sunday morning I went recruiting for volleyball at a tournament at Bethel University. After I was done, I decided to stop at the U and watch the Gopher men play Nebraska, 12:00 tip-off. I did a little shopping on my way out of the cities and drove back to Estherville, had dinner at Woody's Pizza and made some recruit calls from my office. I realize that coaching and recruiting is more of a young person's game, but I am so glad that I am back into coaching again. I am tired as hell today but I am loving life and feeling rejuvenated. Not going to lie, though, I am looking forward to spring break and taking a trip with my wife.

Photo by Mike Turnbull
Gophers vs Nebraska

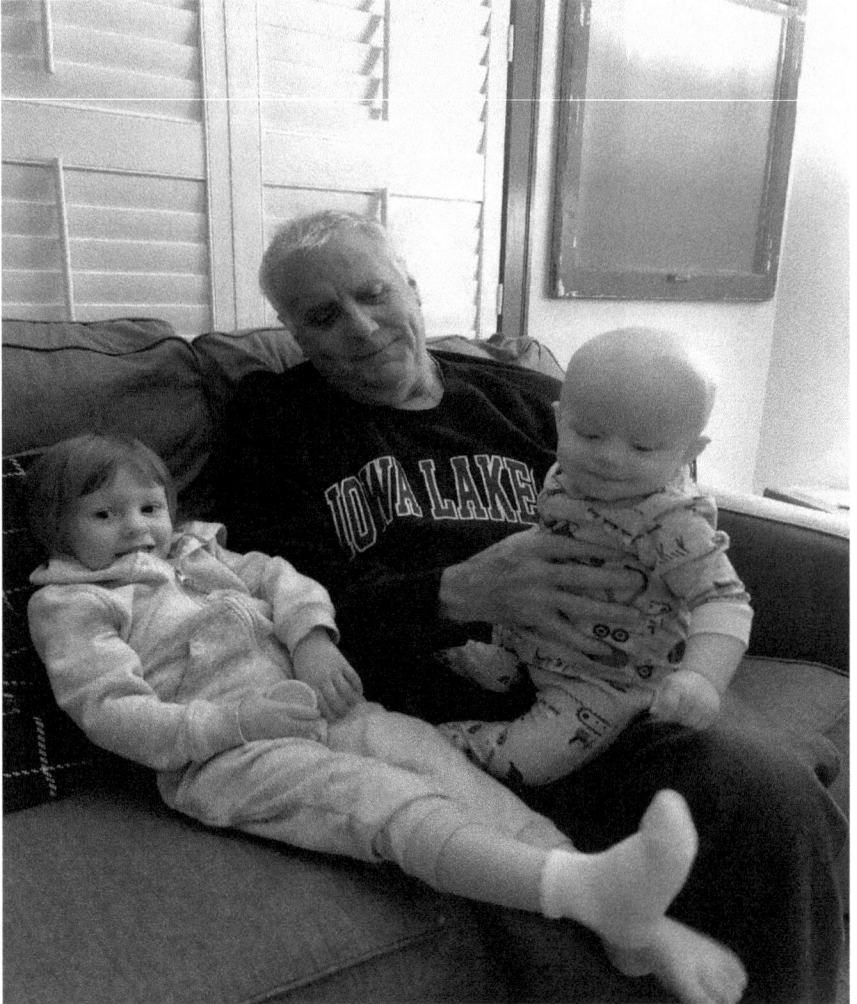

Photo by Alex Turnbull
Brexley, Grandpa Mike, & Hollis
I really do love the whole Grandpa gig!

Just wanted to throw this out there. If I happen to get the Coronavirus and die, make sure someone gets the zip drive out of my computer at work and gives it to my wife. It is either in my office computer or at my desk computer in the Success Center. There is stuff on there I want my wife to have. Pictures, some business information, & notes and copies of this book and others I have written.

My wife and I have been planning on taking a trip to Florida over spring break. Nothing etched in stone, just winging it as usual. Starting to get a little paranoid about traveling. Not pushing the panic button yet but getting more leery by the day.

Today is March 11, 2020. The Coronavirus news really amped up today on the national and local media outlets. Everyone is reacting to and experiencing it in their own personal ways. My wife and I decided to cancel our trip to Florida. We were going to leave tomorrow. I am going to head back to Ely on Friday. We might still take a quick trip to the North Shore of Lake Superior. No tanning on those beaches! I texted a college teammate to tell him we were not coming to Florida to visit. He felt it was a good decision. He didn't think things were going in a good direction in Florida and said he wouldn't be surprised if Disney World closed for a little while. He also told me that his daughter was now stuck in Germany for a month because Trump announced a European travel ban tonight. Here in Iowa, the University of Iowa, Iowa State, University of Northern Iowa and Drake all announced they are all converting to online classes for the next couple of weeks. Nationally: New Rochelle, NY closed entry points, College conference tournaments/NCAA basketball tournament/NBA [no fans], school closings, buffets closing, etc., etc. On the job our school may extend spring break and then decide. My senior apartment building has been basically closed to visitors. God only knows what the next several days will bring. All I can say is, strap it on; it is going to be quite the ride. Pray that logical minds take over. The voice I find myself paying the most attention to right now is the Director of the World Health Organization Tedros Ghebreyesus. If that man told me that peeing in my left ear would keep me healthy, I would do it.

Final note for March 11: My suitcase was packed for Florida; I re-packed for Ely. Out went the shorts, swimsuit, ankle socks, sandals, and sunscreen. In with the sweaters, boots, long pants, knit hats, winter coat, and choppers. Ely is always a safe haven from just about anything except mosquitos, gnats, ticks, and biting flies. I hope it is not too crowded up there. About the only thing that spoils the vibe in Ely is the whole Pro-Mining vs. Environmentalist issues. Still provides entertainment and vibrant discussion if nothing else. Silver lining thoughts: China is almost recovered, I get to go home for a couple of weeks, and I don't have the Coronavirus. Life is good!

I have a question that might fall on deaf and ignorant ears but I will still ask. I saw a commercial for Descovy, which I believe is a medication for HIV prevention. I have seen the commercial twice now. I find the commercial nothing short of confusing. Am I alone on this? One thing I thought I heard was, "Will not work if you were originally assigned as a female." First of all, when did our gender start being assigned? I am pretty sure that I have always been male, but I have never seen any documentation of what gender I was originally assigned. Unless a birth certificate counts? The other thing that I got lost in was all the people in the commercial. There are gays, straights, males, females, and transgender people. I hope to see the commercial again to see if I can figure out who might want to take Descovy.

The panic continues; more cases, more closings and cancelled activities. I am starting to think that title of this book fits perfectly into the COVID-19 Pandemic. Don't be confused, somewhere we switched from Coronavirus to COVID-19. I have heard some people just say "Covid." Still fits: "Observations, Questions, and Very Few Answers." Out of state team travel was banned at our school today. Classes are still scheduled to resume after spring break. I really hoping I am alive to see how the history books record this time. Going home tomorrow; I hope Ely is still a safe haven.

March 26: Still in Ely, not allowed back in Iowa indefinitely. I have to get this off my chest just in case things get out of control. I was cleaning snow off the roof yesterday and my wife offered to help. A lot of snow slid off the roof. Good news, no damage to the new deck. Bad news, haven't been able to find my wife. It is supposed to get up to fifty degrees tomorrow and not too cold tonight, so I hope to find her in the afternoon. I am too tired to keep shoveling tonight. If you see her after all this self-isolation time, forget you ever read this. If I don't find her tomorrow afternoon, forget you ever read this.

I really don't want to talk Pandemic much; we are all dealing with it. One hope that I do have is that when we come out on the other end, people will have a lot more respect for the jobs that we all do. Teachers, doctors, nurses, coaches, cooks, stay at home moms/dads, etc. When normalcy [whatever that will be] returns, I hope parents can go back to being just parents and realize they don't have to try to tell teachers and coaches how to do their jobs. I am looking forward to all of us being able to return to our own lanes in life.

On the community announcements and messages on WELY [Ely radio station] this morning, there was a lost and found message that may have been a complete waste of air time. "Found, hearing aid and face mask outside of the Essentia Clinic. To claim call [xxx] xxx-xxxx." I figure the mask might get claimed but what are the odds on the hearing aid? I hope the owner of the hearing aid has relatives or friends that might have heard the message and can let the owner know.

Our son, daughter-in-law, and grandkids came to Ely for Memorial Day weekend. All I can say is it was special. Beat the hell out of Zoom, Duo, Face time, or phone calls. I can't wait until we can see our daughter, son-in-law, and grandson. I start back to work on Tuesday at Iowa Lakes [May 26], anxious to get a glimpse of the "New Normal."

Photo by Vicki Krouse
Properly social distanced gathering in Winton with friends
Pat & Donna Surface, Dan Krouse
Pam, Vicki, and I served as groupies.

COVID Selfie by Mike Turnbull [I have added to my mask
wardrobe since]

I returned to work yesterday. So far, I am not a big fan of the new normal. I am glad we are taking the steps we are to be safe and healthy, but I am not liking it so far. Pretty sure that is the true definition of a necessary evil. We are wearing masks, social distancing, and calling people around the campus instead of walking over to talk. We are carrying hand sanitizer with us in a little clip-on bottle, and right now only single bathrooms are open. There are still no students on campus yet; classes are online for the summer session. I am sure people all over the country are going through similar experiences of major changes if they are lucky enough to be returning to work.

I have noticed already that most of my fellow employees and I are glad to be back but not really enjoying it yet. It makes me wonder if it is because the environment is so different—or did we get used to working from home?

Watching the local news on television, I have noticed that most of the remote reporters are wearing masks. This new normal may extend the careers of current reporters or open the door for new reporters that actually have faces that were bound for radio.

I coach college volleyball. We still don't know for sure if we are going to have a season this fall. This feeling of the unknown going forward is tough. I don't know how everyone else is dealing with this in their lives but I am just going forward as if our players and students will be back on campus in August and we will have a season. I have always believed in the adage, "Control the controllables and don't worry about what you can't control." Anyone who agrees with that; I know we are all being tested big time right now but be strong and hang in there! I am hoping that Larry Mischke's philosophy is correct, "God takes care of stupid people." I know this "Stupid Man" is still banking on it. [If you are unfamiliar with the "Stupid Man" reference, please check out my previous books.]

What is wrong with this list? Like on Sesame Street, "Which of these doesn't belong?" Minneapolis, Chicago, Atlanta, New York, Los Angeles, Hibbing, & Virginia. All are cities that have had justice for George Floyd protests and lockdown curfews because of unruly behavior of protesters. For those of you who don't know, Hibbing and Virginia are small cities in northern Minnesota.

Several professional athletes have spoken out against George Floyd's murder within a day and are demanding legal justice. There has been completely out of control protests going on for a week. Why aren't these athletes using their platform now to promote peace and respect for property? Nobody in their right mind can think any of the violent protests are helping anything in our country get better right now.

When this pandemic is over there are several phrases I don't want to hear or read for a long time if ever.

"Stay at home."

"Wash your hands."

"You can join the meeting now."

"Maintain a social distance of 6 feet."

"We are all in this together."

"Take out or delivery only."

"Essential employees or businesses."

"The new normal."

"Wear a mask."

"Furloughed or unemployed."

"In these unprecedented times."

"Economic stimulus package."

"Cases have spiked today."

"Cancelled due to Covid-19."

"50% capacity."

"Groups of no more than 6."

"Quarantine"

"Try to maintain some sense of normalcy."

"PPE's"

"By appointment or reservation only."

"Zoom" [I do enjoy pushing the Leave Meeting button.

"Online classes"

"Let's flatten the curve."

"You are not muted!" [In the future will we be saying "Mute yourself" instead of "Shut up"?]

Signs of the "New Normal." Six feet apart is better than six feet under I guess.
Photos by Mike Turnbull

Just picked up some lunch at Casey's and ate outside. It is 95 degrees and sunny today. I was wondering [I do that more than usual lately], now that it is summer in most parts of the country, will there be something new on the horizon? Farmer's tan is pretty common here in Iowa. Are we now also going to see Covid tan? People with pale lower faces and tanned or burnt upper faces.

I have spent several days watching the George Floyd protests from afar and watching and listening to all the talking heads that I can. I thank God I don't live in or have family living in the areas that have been under siege. It hit a little closer to home on Sunday. My son was called into work in downtown Minneapolis. The protesters moved in in front of his building and he was more or less trapped at work a couple blocks away from the ramp he parks on. Anxious several hours for him and his family. I am blessed to say that he did get out and back to his home safely. So, as I said I have been listening to all the talking heads weigh in on the protests. It has left me wondering who could possibly go in front of the angry violent mobs and have a positive impact and turn the situation back to the peaceful protesters and leaders that need to sit down and listen to each other? It has become painfully obvious it is not our President. I would like to suggest Yoda. I came across this quote and I think if he walked through a protest area people would notice. "Fear is the path to the Dark Side. Fear leads to anger, anger leads to hate, and hate leads to suffering."

June 15: Got to watch high school softball and baseball games tonight in Estherville, IA. It was great to see people out enjoying the evening and watching the games. I am really happy for the kids that are lucky enough to get to play because the ISHSL decided to test the waters and start the high school season. To my knowledge, which is limited at best, Iowa is the first state to allow high school sports to resume. I know the whole country is watching to see how it goes. I pray that this proves to be the path forward from some of the Pandemic restrictions. It was heartwarming to see how excited kids were to be out there. I wish major league players would exhibit that kind of love for the game and quit squabbling with owners over the amount of games and pay scales and get their season rolling.

I may have had a breakthrough on mask wearing. I don't think I have removed my mask and thrown my glasses on the ground in about a week. I am finally getting the process down. Take off glasses then the mask. It is like volleyball players; put your knee pads on then your shoes. Goes a whole lot easier.

I have been getting more serious about buying a new truck. I test drove a couple yesterday at Motor Inn in Estherville. I was actually ready to pull the trigger on one today. I wanted to buy one at Mike Motors in Ely but they, sadly, have closed. Anyway, no truck buying today. This morning my wife suggested we hold off a little while. She has a couple more projects at the lake that she wants finished this summer. Don't

51

be fooled by the word "Suggested." That is just wife terminology for "Not going to happen right now."

I have had to make a few trips down to Iowa for work this summer. I have started to take more note of how my life in Northwest Iowa differs from my life in Northeast Minnesota. The following are a few differences that are becoming more obvious.

COVID related:

Masks in public spaces required:
    Iowa = No [HyVee is requiring]/
    Minnesota=Yes

Indoor dining: Iowa = Yes/Minnesota = Limited
    *Iowa is just generally less restricted.

Gas: Iowa = Casey's/
    Minnesota = Holiday or Voyaguer

Groceries: Iowa = HyVee /
    Minnesota = Zup's Grocery

Hardware: Iowa = Bomgaar's/
    Minnesota = Merhar's Ace Hardware

Pizza: Iowa = Woody's or Casey's/
    Minnesota = Sir G's

Movies: Iowa = Grand 3/Minnesota = State Theatre

Big city fix: Iowa = Des Moines/
    Minnesota = Minneapolis-St. Paul

Television News: Iowa = KCAU 9 Sioux City/
    Minnesota = CBS 3 Duluth

Radio: Iowa = Killer Bee 95.9/
    Minnesota = WELY 94.5 or 1450

Local Newspaper: Iowa = Estherville News/
    Minnesota = Ely Echo

Regional Newspaper: Iowa = Des Moines Register/
   Minnesota = Mesabi Tribune

Other noted differences:

Temperature extremes:
   Iowa = 105 degrees [Heat Index]/
   Minnesota = -50 degrees [wind chill]

Income base: Iowa = Farming/
   Minnesota = Mining

Roadside views: Iowa = Corn fields/
   Minnesota = Trees and Lakes

Most likely to see on a large truck trailer:
   Iowa = Pigs/Minnesota = Logs

Most often avoided in the road:
   Iowa = Pheasants and Raccoons/
   Minnesota = Deer

Pro football allegiance:
   Iowa = Vikings and Chiefs [I think the Chiefs is a
   bandwagon thing]/Minnesota = Vikings

Pro baseball allegiance:
   Iowa = Twins, Cubs and Cardinals/
   Minnesota = Twins

Pro hockey allegiance:
   Iowa = [No clue, I think most Iowan's just think
   "Hockey" is a misspelling of "Hawkeye"/
   Minnesota = Wild

College sports allegiance: Iowa = Hawkeyes/
   Minnesota = Gophers

Sport most passionate about:
   Iowa = Wrestling and basketball/
   Minnesota = Hockey

Cause of power outages: Iowa = Wind stops/ Minnesota = Too much wind

My wife and I have taken to watching more Netflix this past spring and summer. I get frustrated when we try to pick a movie. We scroll through and end up coming up with several possibilities after reading descriptions and watching trailers. By the time we tire of this and want to choose a movie I have already forgotten a lot of the movies we have considered 'Maybes." More often than not, when we do start watching a movie we usually don't like it and end up turning it off. Usually we continue watching for a while thinking it will get better. When we finally do give up it is usually too late to start searching again. Every once in a blue moon we get it right and pick a good one.

One of my worst nightmares may have been realized today. I heard on the radio today that the band Abba is making a comeback!

Driving through Iowa today on highway 39 a saw a family of dead raccoons in the road. That is just poor parenting. I honestly think deer and ravens in Minnesota are definitely more responsible with their young.

I have also noticed in my travels throughout Iowa that most small streams are called rivers according to signs. In Minnesota we call them creeks.

What is the difference between a slough and a swamp?

One of the phrases I have heard a lot during the pandemic is; "We are all in this together." I have started to doubt the validity of this statement. The proof is in the pudding [another phrase I don't understand unless it is a Bill Cosby reference]. Anyway, there is a lot going on that refutes the statement "We are all in this together." Protests [violent and peaceful], removal of statues, masks/no masks, Doctor Fauci vs. President Trump, Republicans vs. Democrats, etc. When the Pandemic first started and during lockdown, it was predicted that a lot of babies would be conceived during this time of self-isolating. On the flip side I have become aware, after getting out and socializing a little, of several couples that are getting divorced. They found out they couldn't get along while locked down. I should be done with this book by the time we get by this pandemic but it will be interesting to see the statistics on births and divorces.

Major league baseball began playing again this weekend. I will admit, I never thought it would happen this summer. Gives me hope for sports this fall. I was able to listen to the Twins and White Sox on the radio while driving. I can't explain this but I would rather listen to a game on AM radio as opposed to watching it on television. It really makes drive time fly by and I find something soothing about the poor sound quality. Call me crazy but I think it beats the hell out of high-definition television.

I went to church today with my daughter's family at their church in Nebraska. First time at an in-church service since early March. We have been having church at the United Methodist Church in Ely but it has been in cars and lawn chairs outside in the church parking lot. Today, I was the only one in church wearing a mask. When the Pastor did his sermon, he mentioned that wearing a mask shows love and respect for fellow humans. I didn't look but I am pretty sure a ray of light or a halo appeared above my head. Pretty proud moment for a Methodist attending a Lutheran church service!

There was a report on the news tonight that an Abraham Lincoln statue was vandalized in a park in Sioux City, IA. Parts of it were spray painted red. If that was a form of protest, what was the motive? Some group against tall bearded men? White supremacists against people who favored emancipation? Someone against assassinated Presidents? A group that doesn't like lawyers or perhaps just someone randomly vandalizing park statues? I'll have to do some research on this one to find out if Lincoln is on the politically incorrect list. I did hear this morning that the federal government is considering eliminating the penny from our U.S. currency.

If we get more people back to work and less people self-isolating, will there be fewer mass protests in our city streets? This whole "Anarchists" and "Agitators" thing is really starting to confuse me. It is really hard these days to figure out who the good guys and the bad guys are.

Are we screwed in the U.S. if the vaccine for COVID-19 ends up being discovered in Russia or China? Hopefully the people that say, "We are all in this together" are right.

August 9th, summer is over! I moved back to Iowa today to start the school year at Iowa Lakes CC tomorrow. I had a good last week in Ely. Weed wacked at cut the grass twice. My Aunt and Uncle visited on Thursday and my wife and I took them to eat at the GEL and we went for a pontoon ride on Fall Lake. Friday I umped two baseball games and Pam and I went to the Krause's for dinner. Great dinner and company. Pat and Donna Surface were there also. Pat, Donna, and Dan treated us to some guitar playing and singing. Pam, Vicki, and I provided an appreciative and untalented audience. On Saturday I topped it off by umping two more games and cut the grass again. Pam brought home a Sir G's pizza for dinner. After dinner I took one last bath in the lake. Pam followed that up by cutting my toenails and trimming my eyebrows to make sure I was properly groomed for returning to work. After arriving back in Estherville, I unpacked and stocked up on groceries at Hy-Vee. I topped off my Sunday evening by going to dinner at the Little Swan Lake Winery. I hadn't been there since Pam and I went on Valentine's Day. Dinner was great and the musical entertainment was "Storm Rising." The winery has become one of my favorite live music venues and "Storm Rising," a local band out of Milford, has become one of my favorite acts. Imagine the Lumineers featuring Adele, Etta James, and Patsy Cline. So, as I said, summer is over! Lap swimming and back to work in the morning, ready or not.

Not really sure where it is all going yet in the world of sports, high school on up to the professional levels but the spring of 2021 might be the greatest season of sports ever. There is a strong possibility that just about every major sport may being played this spring all at one time. Not a perfect situation but just think of the binge-watching possibilities! Netflix might even take a hit.

Don't think I mentioned this earlier; I bought a new truck a couple of weeks ago. Shopped around for a few months in three different states and finally found something at Hawkins Chevrolet in Fairmont, MN. The truck is a 2017 Silverado, graded up from my 2011 Sierra. Very happy with it. The day I had to trade in, I was bothered most by having to give up the stickers on my old truck, kind of hit me in the heart. I didn't realize how invested I was in those. Each sticker represented a story in my life. I felt fortunate that I was able to transfer my "COACH T" license plates. New stories will come.

Photo by Mike Turnbull

Photo by Mike Turnbull

Photos by Mike Turnbull

I got my "Tourist" on this past weekend and did some exploring around the Lake Okoboji area this weekend. Saturday I spent some time at Arnold's Park. Toured the Maritime Museum and Amusement Park Museum. Browsed through the Queen's Court shops. I bought Pam a book from the Images of America series, titled "Okoboji and the Iowa Great Lakes." Don't tell her; I haven't given it to her yet and I need to go back to Books-N-Things and get her the "Lost Resorts" book. After Arnold's Park, I went out to Gull Point on West Okoboji and hiked the trails. Overall, Saturday was about the history around the Iowa Great Lakes area. After the hiking I had dinner at Snappers on East Okoboji. My daughter-in-law should be proud of me; I ordered the Avocado BLT. After church on Sunday I decided to go back to Spirit Lake and bring my bike. I have been scouting the bike trails out and I thought it was time to jump in. I started at the fish hatchery in Orleans along Spirit Lake up to Templar Park then back down to downtown Spirit Lake and back to the fish hatchery. Pretty good workout and very scenic. After biking I walked over from the hatchery to the Spillway Drive-In, ordered a root beer float, and took it over to the Orleans Beach and kicked back. I drove into town and hit several antique shops. I felt like I had more biking in me, so I went over to West Okoboji and put in a few miles on the Iowa Great Lakes Trail. I am pretty proud of myself; last summer I had a hip replaced and did no biking, other than stationary. Two summers ago, I couldn't even get my leg over a bike seat. I should have had that hip replaced a few years ago, but again, I did write the "Stupid Man" books. It should be noted, full disclosure, I did get off and walk the bike up one hill. Overall, I was pretty happy with myself. Afterwards I did the cyclist thing and stopped in at the West O Brewery; I love their beer. Topped the day off with dinner at Bracco's on East Okoboji. Great view from the deck, enjoyed my sandwich, but the beer was too expensive. I am starting my second school year working at Iowa Lakes CC and I am feeling less and less like a tourist by the day. The next time my wife comes down, I will have a lot more to show her. I am also really starting to appreciate the history and the beauty of this area. Definitely still have northeast Minnesota in my heart but I am enjoying my time in northwest Iowa.

Photos by Mike Turnbull: Mask collection growing [Maritime Museum, Spillway, and Orleans Beach Okoboji area]

We moved students into the dorms over the weekend and started classes today. I am entering my 40th year of coaching/teaching. When I started my first year out of college in the fall of 1981, I was excited, nervous, and clueless about what I was getting into. You would think those emotions would be different going into my 40th year. With all the unknowns about COVID, the protocol involved in athletics, and the new dynamics on campus, I still feel excited, nervous, and just as clueless as I did that first fall. I shared these sentiments with my wife. She said I was wrong. She added, "In 1981 you were cocky and naive enough to think you had all the answers. Now you are old enough to realize you are clueless."

I had my first meeting with my volleyball team tonight. A little weird, socially distanced and in Pods. First impressions: I really like them. We have some unique personalities. I was surprised to see how connected they are already even though this was their first face to face meeting outside of their Pods. We will be conditioning and socializing in Pods for the next two weeks. Now we have to just stay healthy moving forward. We also have to slow our roll because we don't play until January. This is a big change! The normal is come in, start practicing, and begin playing in about two weeks. This year we have 4 ½ months to get ready for the season. I am just thankful we might get the opportunity to have a season.

Prayer of confession at church today: Loving God, we sit in the ashes of our hopes, but you see us as your beloved children. We pay attention to all who break the rules, but ignore the grace that is poured out upon us. We try to box you in with boundaries we can manage, but you continue to burst forth to bring newness into the world. Have mercy on us, God of forgiveness, and open our eyes to your presence among us. As you look at our hearts, may we see others in a different way, not as enemies or strangers, but sisters and brothers of the same family, kin to Jesus Christ, our lord and savior. Amen

I am not enjoying watching television much these days. Other than the news, I tend to use television as an escape from daily life. Lately there is no getting away from it. COVID-themed commercials and political campaign commercials. Even when I flip to ESPN it seems like every athlete interview or highlight video makes reference to social injustice or get out and vote message. I really hope all these causes don't get lost in the overkill. So where does the truth lie in all this rhetoric? I have been searching for information delivered by someone who is not trying to sell a product or get elected. So far the search has been fruitless. I have come to realize the truth is found in the same place it has been all my life, at church and in the Bible.

When it comes to mask wearing, opening schools, or allowing copper-nickel mining in the Ely area; my answer is the same: trust the science.

Please indulge me on this one, because I really don't know where I am going with this. I am just going to start writing and let my thoughts take their own course. Back to my author roots, "Random Thoughts of a Stupid Man." My wife called this afternoon. I took the call in my coach's office. She first asked if I had found some documents, we had both been looking for a while now. Of course, I had not. She had, so I really don't know why she asked, other than to check if I had looked. Pam went on to tell me that Becky Ode had called in the morning and they had talked for about an hour. Pam and Becky tend to ramble when they see each other or talk on the phone, especially Becky. I asked her how things were going with Bud, Becky, and their family. Pam's voice broke and she said, "Not good." Instinctively, my thoughts turned to Bud. Not so odd, I had been thinking about calling Bud last week to check in. Unfortunately, I let life get in the way and put it off. Pam regained her composure and said, "Bud passed away on Saturday night." After hearing the details, I had a gut-wrenching cry in my office. Luckily, most of the people in my office suite had left for lunch. I think I have only been hit emotionally this hard twice in my life, after my dad and mom passed. There is something harder though about no forewarning or preparation. Bud was at my dad's funeral and called shortly after my mom passed. I can easily say Bud was right there with my mom and dad when it comes to influential people in my life. Let me explain. Bud came into my life in the fall of 1981 and I was fortunate enough to have this man in my life for 40 years. Actually, longer than I shared this life with my dad; I was 30 when he passed. In 1981 I started my teaching and coaching career in Lake Park, MN. I was three months out of college and hired as a social studies teacher, head boys' basketball coach, and assistant volleyball coach at the high school. Shortly after arriving in Lake Park, I was told by a teaching colleague that Bud Ode wanted to meet me. I quickly learned that I was preparing to meet the equivalent of the "Godfather" in Lake Park. Many locals affectionately referred to Bud as "Buddha." Fitting nickname for many reasons. Bud was obviously a local legend in Lake Park, up and down Highway 10 and in northwest Minnesota. After soaking all this in, I finally mustered the courage to go up to "The Shop" and meet Bud. Bud owned and operated Bud's Sports Center on Highway 10 just outside of Lake Park. I am not sure what it was for sure, but Bud and I hit it off right away. I would go as far to say, "kindred spirits." Of course, a love of sports was a common thread, but there was more to it. I asked Bud if he would be willing to be my assistant basketball coach if the school board approved. I had been hired to coach the A, B, and C squads and the superintendent had said they hoped to get an assistant by Christmas. I am pretty sure Bud got that to happen earlier than that. On the basketball end we collaborated with an outstanding group of players and finished the season winning Lake Park's, first ever District Championship. I don't think any of us knew where that season was going when it started, but it was a great ride! I appreciated Bud immensely at the time, but as the years have passed that appreciation has grown into a deep admiration, gratefulness, and a realization that I was truly blessed to have Bud in my life. I know I never told him, [he probably would have slapped me] but, I loved him like a dad. I want Becky, Jody, Jana, and other family members to know that. I would have to write another book to list all the things that Bud provided in my life that I am grateful for. I believe God, in his infinite wisdom, brought us together in 1981. Our lives have geographically distanced over the years but never mentally or emotionally. You don't know how bad I wish I had called him last week when I was thinking about him. I also feel torn because I can't attend the funeral. I am back at work in Iowa and trapped in the "bubble" by COVID restrictions and no outstate travel. Bud, that means there will be two extra sandwiches for somebody at lunch. I have had a successful career as a teacher/coach and I feel I have a few more years left in the tank. I have been happily married for almost 39 years and I think I am doing a good job as a father, father-in-law, and grandpa. I have a wife who still loves me, wonderful adult children, I am blessed with a great son- and daughter in-law, and I have three grandchildren I absolutely cherish. I'm not saying that Bud is responsible for all of this, but Pam and I will both tell you that Bud and Becky were and are instrumental in helping us navigate our adult lives. Married life, parenting, grand parenting, balancing family life, and work, etc., etc. As far as coaching goes, I may never had made it through those early years without Bud's guidance. The Lake Park community was a great place to start a career, but I might have gotten eaten alive without Bud guiding me through the ups and downs. I will never know what he did to keep the wolves off my back as we figured it out together. I do know that my career may never have played out the way it has without him laying the foundation and nurturing me over the years.

Becky has always been the cheerleader and positive energy in our live. Bud was/is the rock. My daughter was born early in the morning on May 11, 1983 in Detroit Lakes. Becky wanted me to take Polaroid pictures of Lexie so I could share them when I came home that night. My first stop was the Ode house. Becky, Jody, and Jana all gushed over the pictures. Bud looked at the pictures and said, "Yep, looks like a baby to me" and headed downstairs to watch the news. That is the Bud that I will always love, respect, and miss! Ironic that a weak heart is what eventually was his demise. I believe it is because he gave so much heart to his life's endeavors and the people in it. I can only hope that when my time is done on this earth that someone will remember me this fondly. Readers: Thanks for taking the time to indulge me. ~ Mike Turnbull ~

The COVID-19 Pandemic may alter the definitions of some words forever. Examples:

WORD	Previous Definition	Going Forward
Red State	Republican State	COVID cases are spiking
Homesick	Missing home	Want to get out of isolation
Normal	The same as always	Mask wearing, social distancing, etc.
Corona	Beer	Disease
Donald Trump	U.S. President	Ex-President?

*Feel free to continue this list as you wish.

One of my favorite childhood Christmas songs was "All I want for Christmas is my two front teeth"; maybe someone more talented than me can rewrite the lyrics this year. "All I want for Christmas is a COVID vaccine." I know it wouldn't be as sexy, but maybe Mariah Carey could rework her classic Christmas song also.

With NBA and NHL play-offs starting to wrap up it has been interesting to watch the ends of play-off series. In a normal year they talk about the disappointment of having to go home. This year the losing teams know that they can leave their respective "bubbles" and that going home, is a good thing.

I have heard talk of possible television show reboots. I would like to pitch a "Seinfeld" reboot or reunion show. It could be COVID based. I am guessing that Elaine and Kramer would be terrible about mask wearing. The producer could do a scene where the two of them refuse to wear masks. Elaine would have a vanity issue and Kramer just wouldn't be able to physically keep one on. A masked Soup Nazi could say, "No mask, no soup for you!" Jerry, Newman, & George would most likely be mask wearers. Newman might have breathing issues.

We got word of our first positive COVID test on our volleyball team today. First concern, the player that tested positive and her health. Second, her room mates, who are also team mates. Next, the rest of the team and lastly, myself. We will suspend practices, do some quarantining and isolating, and go from there with whatever Public Health tells us. The key now is to just pause and be calm. Control the controlables, for whatever that is worth. Anxiety levels are definitely amped up. Time, science, our administrators, athletic protocol, and the Iowa State Health Department will guide the process. I am definitely not ruling out prayers for all the best! I still can't believe there are people that think this COVID thing is a hoax. I am also glad the NJCAA had the foresight to push athletic competition to the spring. Odds are we'll have a couple more cases on the team as we move forward. I am confident that things will be okay when we come out at the other end of this Pandemic, but I really have no idea what the end game really is. Everyone just needs to just stay the course. I pray that when we all get through this and tell our COVID stories years from now that we are only talking about 2020-21.

Rough week on the volleyball front but turned out okay. We added a player for second semester, one step forward. Two steps backward, lost a player. She went home due to financial problems. One player out with Tonsilitis, one step sideways. One player isolated with COVID symptoms, another step sideways. She tested negative and will return Monday, one step to the right. As far as I can tell this all leaves us one step back, not bad. Next week we get a player back from quarantine on Tuesday and two back on Friday. Can only hope that COVID-19 leaves us alone for a while. One of the other teams on campus can take a turn. I am getting way to comfortable chatting with people from Public Health about tracing. I really miss the days of just having to worry about academic eligibility for our student-athletes.

Side note: I am not complaining, I am the one who voluntarily came out of retirement to coach again. I hope that all this COVID crap doesn't scare too many coaches out of the profession.

Crazy evening at the Little Swan Lake Winery tonight. If you read anything about a COVID spike in Superior, IA this is when and where it came from. LSL Winery has dinner and live music from 4 to 6:00 on

Sundays. I love going out there. Dinner never disappoints and the entertainment is top notch. Tonight's music was Dave & Ryan. Started out just fine; Billy Joel, Mel Torme, Elton John, Jimmy Buffet, Tom Petty, CCR, and Johnny Cash covers. A little after 5:00 they played "500 Miles" and the audience started firing up. Then they did a few Irish Pub tunes and it got more wired in the room. Keep in mind the audience is mostly 50+ and most are over 60 years old. The seating was socially distanced at tables, but still a little tight. Some mask wearing. I was by myself and masked. [Just saying.] At about 5:30 Dave & Ryan played "Play that Funky Music Whiteboy." The floor space became filled with dancers. It looked like something out of the "Cocoon" movie. The world is officially out of control, even in small town NW Iowa. If Public Health calls me about tracing, I will be able to say I left at about 5:35.

Why doesn't Estherville have calendar parking? If they do, why isn't it enforced?

The Washington Redskins have to change their name and the Cleveland Indians had to drop Chief Wahoo. These movements toward politically correct names and mascots hasn't hit Iowa yet. Friday night I watched a high school football game between the ELC Midgets and the Spirit Lake Indians. Last night I went volleyball recruiting and watched the Pocahontas Indians play the Clarion-Goldsmith-Dows Cowgirls. I am not complaining, there is a lot of entertainment value in watching Midgets and Indians/Indians and Cowgirls get after it and compete. Beats the heck out of

Lions and Bengals or Tigers and Blue Jays.

Great weekend, my wife was finally able to come down to Iowa and visit. I have been stuck here in the "bubble" since August 9th, so it has been about two months. I have a visitor log sheet in my apartment for tracing purposes. She was the first visitor to sign in other than the cleaning lady. Visitors have to submit their name, phone number, and reason for visiting. My wife, in her infinite wisdom, entered "Conjugal." I appreciated her humor but got her to change it to "Wife." Anyway, nice weekend. We went out to dinner a couple of times, spent a day in Arnold's Park, and hit a Big Band concert at the Roof Garden. Sunday, breakfast at Bud's Café, more time around the Okoboji area, and dinner and music at the Little Swan Lake Winery. "Storm Rising" was the band; love them! Little calmer crowd than the Dave & Ryan night. Pam went home on Monday and I hope to see her again later in October. We'll meet in the cities and help our son and his family move into their new home in the cities.

Photo by Mike Turnbull: Proof to the people of Estherville that Pam is not imaginary and she was in town.

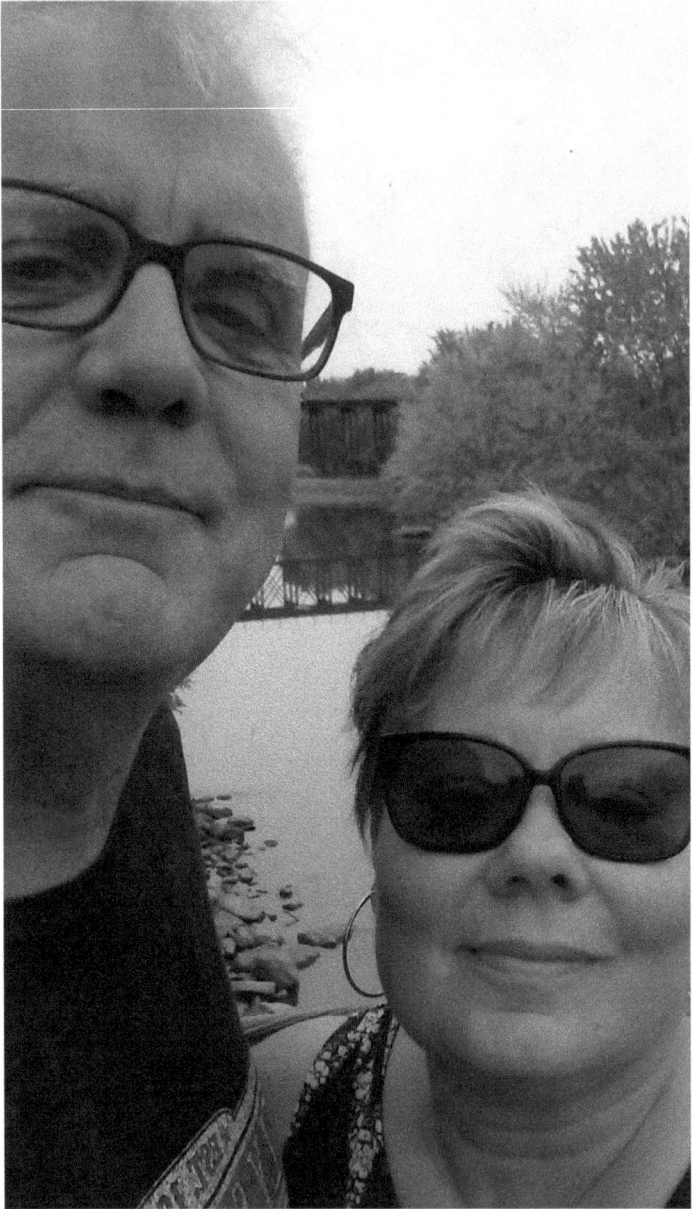

Photo by Pam Turnbull: Swinging Bridge in Estherville, IA

Big week for our volleyball team. We are back to full strength and get to scrimmage SWICC next week.

I am anxious to see them in live playing conditions.

First Presidential debate last night, wow? What the hell was that? I feel bad for anyone that tuned in expecting to witness a debate. If something doesn't change, I don't know why they should bother with the next two debates. I can go to any bar and listen to two old guys argue and interrupt each other.

I heard today that changes to the Presidential debate rules are being considered, such as muted microphones after two minutes or when out of order. I think they should just have an old nun or kindergarten teacher moderate the debates. I can't think of any man in his right mind that would buck either one.

We scrimmaged SWICC yesterday. It went well; I have never seen a team in my 40 years of coaching so excited to scrimmage someone. The COVID Pandemic has definitely inspired an appreciation for things that we normally take for granted in our lives. I know I was glad to see the joy they played with and we played well to top it off.

Now I am pissed; someone stole the "Life is Good" hitch cover off my truck. That is just wrong on so many levels. I feel violated! I was parked in a lot in Sprit Lake. I hope whoever stole it plans to use it. It is a message that needs to be continued to be shared.

My sister let me know today that she and my brother-in-law are cancelling the family Thanksgiving at their house due to COVID concerns. It is a good call on their part. Our family gathers every year, always have, but there is no sense in risking our health this year. We would be gathering in the Twin Cities and coming in from Ely, MN, Austin, MN, Estherville, IA, Chicago, IL, southern California, Nebraska, and Phoenix, AZ with family members that live in the Minneapolis area. Try tracing that breakout. It would be worse than a Trump "Super Spreader" event. I have missed one family Thanksgiving in my life. In 1981, my first year of teaching, I got stuck in a blizzard in Lake Park, MN and couldn't get back to Ely. We'll see what my wife decides to do now. Instead of spending it with the Turnbulls, Rahjas, Jennings and Baacks, we'll be with the Loes and LaTourells most likely.

I have yet to completely buy into the Las Vegas Raiders. I have been a Raiders' fan since 1965. Hard to accept the Las Vegas move. The LA years were tough but they fixed that. I am glad they didn't change the logo or colors. I am glad to see John Gruden succeed but he has gotten fat. Too many Vegas buffets, maybe?

Yesterday was Columbus/Indigenous Peoples Day. Saw a few more statues knocked down on the news. I started wondering, with people becoming more concussion aware and all the deaths that are being attributed to CTE, our society is becoming negative about high impact sports such as football and boxing. We might eventually do away with those sports. If these sports are something that we eventually look back on and determine as barbaric, dangerous, and something we shouldn't have done, will people be tearing down statues of famous boxers and football players? Will we demolish the Boxing and Football Hall of Fames?

It has been a tough couple of weeks for some of my boyhood sports heroes. I have been saddened by the deaths of Gayle Sayers, Bob Gibson, Whitey Ford, and Joe Morgan. I idolized and emulated all of them growing up.

Closer to home, Bob McDonald passed away yesterday. A lot of people will remember him as the winningest high school basketball coach in Minnesota. I hope some can remember that he coached for 59 years. That will never be duplicated! I have coached for forty and I do not have plans for coming anywhere near 59. Most importantly, I hope Bob is remembered fondly by those boys that he coached and mentored to transition from boys to men. I will remember him as a friend and mentor.

I have been receiving emails from Microsoft, from something called "Cortana." I am relatively sure that Cortana is a woman. Just assuming because, Alexis, Siri, Cortana, it fits. Anyway, I unsubscribed; she scares me & threatens any sense of privacy I have. She reads my emails at night and then sends me messages in the morning reminding me to take care of things I may have mentioned in previous day's emails. I have a wife, three sisters, a daughter, a daughter-in-law, a granddaughter, a mother-in-law, and five female supervisor/bosses at work. Not to mention my mom's voice of reason that exists in my head and heart. To top it off, I coach a college women's volleyball team. My point here, is that I have more than enough women in my life reminding me of things to do or advising and directing me. If any of them are not around, the women in my apartment building keep tabs on me also. I cannot unsubscribe to any of them. Cortana gave me the option of unsubscribing so I took it; hopefully it sticks but I have a suspicion she may still be reading my emails. The rest of the women in my life will stay, subscription or not, because I respect and love them all. I just have no room to add Cortana to my life; besides, she kind of freaks me out.

Speaking of women in my life, there are a few I would like to thank. These women probably don't realize but they make my day complete almost every day of the week. Their smiles and kind words go a long way on a typical day.

6:30 AM Don't know her name; The computer that says "Welcome" when I check in at the RWC for lap swimming.

7:10 AM Abbi the lifeguard says, "Have a nice day."

8:00 AM Sarah says, "Good morning and how are you?" in the athletic/housing office.

8:05 AM Angie & Molly greet me with good mornings and silly songs in the library/success center.

11:30 AM Sandy comes to work and says, "Good morning and how was your evening?"

5:50 PM Volleyball team answering COVID screening questions and telling me about their day before we start practice.

9:15 PM Phone call home to my wife. We talk about our days and exchange "I love yous & goodnights."

10:30 PM Sophie Erber signs off on the Channel 9 News.

7:30 AM November 3, 2020: Just got back to my apartment after lap swimming. Huge day ahead for all of us! I have already voted so I don't have to worry about that today. I really don't know who is going to win this thing. I am not a political analyst or a pollster but I have been observing some behaviors that might indicate how people will vote. Examples: People who crowd your COVID social space = Trump. People diligently wearing masks = Biden. People wearing masks when they are driving alone = Probably won't vote. The guy that leaves a public bathroom without washing their hands = Trump. The person with the grocery cart full of toilet paper, hand sanitizer, Cheetos, and Keystone Light beer = Undecided. The guy in the voting booth next to you wearing a gun = Trump. People chanting "Lock her up!" = Trump. People that believe global warming and the Pandemic are a hoax = Trump. I am not sure what the indicator would be for Kanye voters; possibly severe brain trauma.

I am extremely alarmed that the national news has been showing scenes of cities all over the country that are boarding up, barricading, and bringing in extra security, in anticipation of protests, rioting, and looting after the election is decided. I think they should also be prepared for the angry mobs of people that will lose their minds waiting for all the ballots to be counted and the announcement of a winner. I think we will probably tire of the phrase, "Too close to call." Even the White House has an additional protective barrier in place. Nobody is talking about what result may produce what reaction. Fence and walls are always put in place to keep someone in or out. The fence around the White House; are we trying to keep someone in or out? So much for peaceful transfer of power, which we as Americans have always prided ourselves on. Be healthy and hopeful!

Wednesday, November 4, 11:00 PM: Electoral vote count has not changed all day. "Too close to call." I don't know if this is an indicator of social priorities or not, but here goes. As of 11:00 PM CST, the Presidential race has not been decided. Arizona, Montana, South Dakota, and New Jersey have all legalized recreational marijuana. "Bada Boom-Bada Bong"! Mississippi and South Dakota also approved medicinal marijuana use. South Dakotans have it all covered now. Oregon decriminalized possession of small amounts of heroin and cocaine. Colorado instituted a bill de-felonizing possession of user amounts of heroin, cocaine, and methamphetamine. Starting in March, just a misdemeanor. I know the Pandemic has hit us all hard, but "Come on Man!" The question that begs an answer, "What is the end game?"

I still want to know how Panda Express stays in business. I thought Pandas were a protected species. I have never eaten at a Panda Express. Does Panda meat taste like chicken?

Every once I awhile I catch a television commercial about the "Bachelorette." The host says, "Congratulations you have just blown up the Bachelorette." Not that I am losing sleep over it, but what happened?

The last two nights watching several television networks covering election results, I have heard the phrase, "The ballot counters continue to work tirelessly around the clock," several times. Unless you are superwoman or superman you have to be getting tired if you are working around the clock.

Okay, North Dakota wins the strange election results contest. They elected a state representative that died of COVID complications in early October. That is just poor tracing by the public health department. Nice to see people coming together to fight back against COVID though.

The other day I was searching the internet for some inspirational quotes to share with my volleyball players. The subject I chose was "The light at the end of the tunnel." I would like to share a few with you.

"Believe there is a light at the end of the tunnel. Believe you might be that light for someone else. ~ Kobi Yamada ~

"Maybe the light is at the other end of the tunnel." ~ Ben Fountain ~

"You have to fight through some bad days to earn the best days of your life." ~ Anonymous ~

"Sometimes that light at the end of the tunnel is a train." ~ Charles Barkley ~

My personal favorite: "I got tired of waiting for the light at the end of the tunnel and lit that bitch up myself!" ~ Snarky Quotes Journal ~

I am 61 years old now and I become acutely aware that eventually we do become our parents. I have drawn comparisons to my dad for years. I recognize some of them. I do know that I am not as patient as my dad was. I am patient, but I think that my patience and tolerance level pales in comparison to my dad's. In my defense, I think my RA has something to do with that. Not a very rational thought, my dad had RA and eventually Cancer. He passed away at 53. I do think he would be proud of how I have navigated the COVID Pandemic up to this point. I am glad that he and my mom are not here to deal with it. I know that sounds bad but that is how I feel. All that said, today I was thinking I may also be turning into my mother. Today is Wednesday and I stopped at the grocery store for the third time this week. That makes Monday, Tuesday, and today. My mom would understand. I know people who knew her, know what I am talking about. When my family lived in Ely, she stopped at Zup's and Joe's IGA on a daily basis. Later, when she lived in the cities and still had her health, she was a regular visitor to Rainbow, Cub, and Byerly's. My mom also worked at a grocery store at times. I don't see that happening for me but I am not ruling it out. When I am done coaching in Iowa and get back to Ely on a permanent basis maybe I can be a night stocker at Zup's or maybe Denny will give up his job at Northland Market. In the meantime, I will try to stay out of Hy-Vee tomorrow.

Blake Shelton said something on "The Voice" the other day that has me lying awake at night wondering about it, because I refuse to ask Google for an answer. He said, "Why do they call them a Unicorn? Unihorn would make more sense." I think I just got my answer: my computer wants to spell check Unihorn.

It has been a very long week separated from my volleyball team. We have two players quarantining at their apartment and the rest of us had to lay low and take a pause from practice. Don't tell my players, I don't want them to think I am getting soft, but I miss them. Seeing them at the end of the day for practice is the best part of my day. Hopefully, we can get back at it next week. The disconnect is not good for any of us.

Photo by Mike Turnbull
Front L-R Mady Brevik, Hannah Main, Kylie Kline
Back L-R Jacklyn Dean, Quiana Coria-Lopez, Hope Serra-
no, & BrookLynn Anderson
Not pictured: Dania Ponce-Diaz

I have gotten back to simple pleasures. I was home for the first time since August. The Winton Roadhouse is open again. New name, HD Winton Roadhouse, but very much the same. I hope Hailey and Dave can keep it going. Woody's Pizza in Estherville has been open for indoor dining for a few weeks. Vikings' games, two Shiner Bock's, and a small pepperoni pizza on Sundays, nice! Also, now that winter has kicked in, who would have ever guessed how comforting the heated leather seats in my new truck are. Sometimes, I sit in the parking lot and enjoy, if I get to work early.

My email at work got hacked today. The technology department said I should change my password. This definitely throws a little more stress into my life; I had just locked my password to memory and now I have to create a new one. We have 18-character passwords! Who, in their right mind uses 18-character passwords? Also, do hackers have absolutely no regard for fellow human beings?

Note to hackers: There is a fricking Pandemic still going on and Donald Trump will not concede the election! Why don't you people put your computer skills to good use and do some COVID tracing for your local health department or at the very least, count ballots!

Who would have ever guessed that the Ivy league and the NJCAA would be on the same wave length? The Ivy League cancelled fall sports. The NJCAA moved all sports to spring semester. Today the Ivy League became the first Division 1 League to postpone winter sports, thy are considering February. Right now, after seeing what has happened in college sports this fall, I would say that the Ivy League and the NJCAA got it right putting competition off to the spring and that is no guarantee. Could it possibly be because the Ivy League and the NJCAA are not chasing the money or profit margin?

Fellow males, I have a suggestion or an excuse for you to consider, depending on your motivation. We can all help with the flattening of the COVID curve if we all leave toilet seats up. If we all get on board with this, we can reduce the amount of contacts touching the seat. I have tried to check this idea with the CDC and they haven't responded. I might try Dr. Fauci next. I'll get back to you on this. In the meantime, unite with me and leave the toilet seats up. Warning: if your wife is like mine, she might be hesitant to get on board with this movement. Be strong!

How many new stadiums have opened basically empty this year? Two that I know of, the Texas Rangers' stadium in Arlington and the S0-Fi stadium in Los Angeles that houses the Chargers and Rams. I think this spring the Golden State Warriors will also open a relatively empty arena, sad.

I have mentioned anti-PC nicknames at Iowa High Schools at other points throughout this book, add one more. I recruited a player from Wapello. The nickname for the boy sports' teams is "Indians"; for the girls' teams it is "Arrows." I have no idea why.

Pastor Moore was on vacation this week, so lay leader Jan Lange did the sermon. She was outstanding as usual. She delivered a Veterans' Day themed sermon. Among other topics, she discussed four necessaries for surviving hard times. Considering where we are at these days, I took notes for anything I could share with my players. These were the four points she made and backed them up with scripture. 1] Be strong! 2] Commit! 3] Endure! 4] Stay focused!

I have raveled a lot this fall recruiting and have a lot of alone time in the evenings. I try to make a point of calling or texting random contacts in my phone to reach out to and check their well-being. I just do those I haven't had any contact with for a while. It has been great reconnecting with people I haven't heard from or of for quite some time. I shouldn't have waited until a Pandemic to start doing this. I know people would argue with me but I feel it beats the hell out of Facebook.

I would like to share a story that I believe I first heard told by Coach Lou Holtz at a coaches' clinic. I have heard it told in various versions a few times over the years. I have used it several times with my teams at the beginning of seasons. I apologize for not being able to credit the originator of the story. "Anonymous" gets used way to often and gets too much credit. I am going to have to add one more to his/her list of credits.

A wealthy rancher/oil baron in Texas hosted his annual summer barbecue for family, friends, employees and business colleagues. I was lucky enough to be one of the random guests he also invites on occasion. The ranch was similar to "Southfork" in the Dallas television show. After dinner had been served and consumed, our host invited all of us to meet him by the Olympic size pool behind the main house. The pool was filled with sewage, weeds, alligators, piranhas, and poisonous snakes. Our host held up a check for one million dollars. He said, "I will give this check to anyone who is brave enough to swim in and swim from one end of the pool to the other." As he continued to speak, there was a splash in the pool. The guests rushed to the edge of the pool and began to cheer. The young man in the pool began to kick and paddle his way across the pool. At times he disappeared below the surface, for what seemed to be an eternity. Each time he came back to the surface and resumed fighting his way through the pool. He punched and kicked alligators, grabbed snakes and thew them out of the pool, and kept pulling piranhas off his body. The guests crowded up around all edges of the pool and wildly cheered him on. He finally got to the far end of the pool and climbed out. He pulled any remaining piranhas off his body and threw them back in the pool. He wiped off the weeds and sewage and tried to spit out anything he had spoiled. The guests went crazy congratulating him until the host stepped up. "Young man, I have presented this challenge to my barbecue guests for the past fifteen years. Nobody has even been brave enough to enter the pool. You have shown us all an unsurpassed level of bravery, courage and strength. Before I give you the million dollars, do you have any words of wisdom you would like to share with all of us?" The young man took the check, looked around at all the other guests and said, "Yes I would. Who the hell pushed me in the pool?"

We have all been pushed in the pool in 2020. I hope and pray we all get to climb out on the other end. I plan to be there. I won't have a million dollars for you. Pretty sure there are no more stimulus checks coming. My hope is that we can just take the masks off, share some long hugs, and celebrate the fact that we made it and honor and remember those who did not!

Be safe, healthy, & hopeful.
Happy Thanksgiving!

Photo by Mike Turnbull: Definitely better days ahead!

Photo by Lexie Baack: Be thankful you didn't get a COVID haircut from my daughter. My grandson Beckett was the only one to suffer that fate.

Photo by Mike Turnbull: I am truly blessed!

Photo by Mike Turnbull: Ready to go; hats, gloves, coat, and COVID masks!

AFTERWORD

I started reading "Washington's End" by Jonathan Horn this summer. I am almost done. It has been a great read but tough to digest. I have backed up and read several times.

One thing I have learned is that George Washington wrote letters to his young nephews on a daily basis. I do not write with the eloquence or wisdom that Washington wrote with but I thought I might enjoy doing that with my grandchildren. I haven't started doing it yet, maybe in 2021? As a dry run, I will make my first attempt now.

Photo by Alex Turnbull

Dear Beckett,

I hope this letter finds you happy and healthy. Your Grammy and I are very excited about coming to your house for Thanksgiving this year. I know it will be very different but I hope we get to pull it off.

I want you to know how much we miss you. We think of you and pray for your well-being every day. I know we don't get to see each other as much as we would like but we know that you and your mom and dad have a good life in Nebraska and that brings us peace.

It has not been perfect coaching in Iowa and being away from Grammy for long periods of time either. I have enjoyed being able to see you more often than waiting for you to come to Ely or us finding time to travel to Nebraska. I really enjoyed it when you came to visit me in Iowa on Labor Day weekend and we got to go to Arnold's Park. I hope you liked your time here.

This is a huge year in your life. Grammy and I are very proud of how well you are doing in Kindergarten. We have always known you are a smart kid and you are definitely proving it. I know it has been difficult being in and out of school with COVID restrictions, but you are doing a great job! When you are at home, continue to trust and cooperate with your mom and dad. They are both good teachers also. I don't know if you know this but your mom has an elementary education degree.

Photo by Lexie Baack

I was very proud to hear that your teacher reported that you are respectful of her and your classmates. She also said you show a high level of empathy. That will go a long way for you and is exactly what we need more of in this world right now. Grammy and I were also glad to hear that you want to learn to play the piano and you want your mom to teach you. That is great; maybe your Uncle Blaine can help you too!

I know a lot of your other activities have been cancelled during the Pandemic. I really hope you will be able to get back to those in the near future. I am not thrilled about soccer but I know you enjoy it and are good at it. I will support you in any activities you participate in. Nothing wrong with broadening your horizons.

Oh yeah, your mom and dad tell me you have two girlfriends. First, five years old is too young for girlfriends. Second, I don't care how old you are, the two girlfriends at once thing is never going to end well for you. Just saying!

As you get older and have more things going on in your life, it will be harder for you to get up to Fall Lake and Ely in the summer. I don't want to throw a guilt trip on you, we'll leave that up to your Grammy, but that time with you is very special to us and I hope we can find a way to continue to make that happen. I am also looking forward to getting back to the College World Series in Omaha with you. In about sixteen years from now we can have a beer together at the Happy Bar between games.

I also want you to know that whenever your Grammy and I get around to writing our will, we are going to leave the house at Fall Lake to your mom and uncle. I hope you will be traveling up to Ely and enjoying life at the lake for many years to come.

I don't know if you are aware yet but your mom has decided to stop coaching for now so she can spend more time with you and your dad. You probably won't notice until next fall, it will be a good thing!

I really hope you continue to appreciate your mom and dad. They work very hard and want all the best for you, as we all do. Always know that you are loved by your family in Nebraska and your family in Minnesota. Keep being you, we all know there are great things coming on your horizon. See you next week!

Love, Grandpa

Photo by Lexie Baack

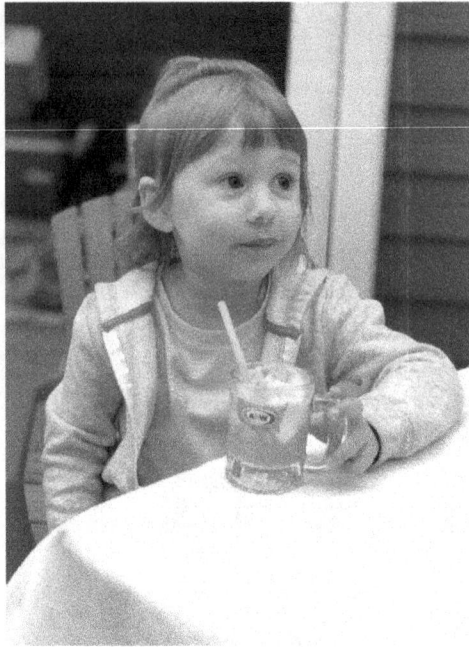

Photo by Alex Turnbull: Our favorite granddaughter Brexley

Dear Brexley,

You are only three and have had such an impact on us all. You are a special kid, full of energy and personality. You are definitely headed to a leadership role down the road. I am confident you will do all kinds of good things in this world.

I hope you are getting settled into your new house and neighborhood and taking care of your little brother. I also hope you are doing everything you can do to help your mom and dad with the unpacking and moving in process.

I am sure it hasn't been easy being at a new day care either. I am glad to hear you are making new friends and helping Hollis with the transition also. Be sure to always listen to the Day Care ladies and do as they say. Never forget how important it is to be patient, share, and wait your turn. You will not always be able to get your way. I know that you are working on this but it is not an easy listen. Do not let it stress you too much; I know somewhere in the future you will be the one in charge and calling the shots.

Moving to your new house has not been easy on your mom or dad either. They have added stress at their jobs with changes the Pandemic has caused. Please be patient with them and help around the house whenever you can.

Photo by Alex Turnbull

Your Grammy and I have been really happy to have been able to see you and Hollis a few times this fall. We think your new house is beautiful! Both of you bring joy to our hearts. Actually, some of the things you do crack us up. I do a little better job of hiding that than your Grammy.

Photo by Alex Turnbull

Just always know how much we love and adore you! You are a lucky young girl. Not all kids are blessed as you. You have two parents that love you and each other. You have two sets of loving grandparents. Bonus: Both sets of grandparents own lake homes. You have a little brother that adores you and needs you. You have family on both sides that love you and are looking forward to great things out of you.

Grammy and I are looking forward to seeing you in Nebraska for Thanksgiving. Travel safely; we'll see you there. Your cousin Beckett is fired up you are coming to his house. Hopefully, he will get to see your new house this summer.

Love you,

Love Grandpa

Photo by Alex Turnbull: Hollis' First Birthday

Dear Hollis,

Your first full year on this earth has been a heck of a ride. In suspect in the future you will have no memory of the COVID Pandemic, just a lot of weird pictures to look at. Your socially distanced birthday party and several pictures of people in masks or masks hanging off their ears. I am happy for you that most businesses and events require masks for people over the age of two. You have it made, continue to milk it but do try to stick to the handwashing and social distancing.

You did get to spend a lot of time at home with your mom, dad, and Brexley; you may not know it but that was a good thing. Beats the heck out of Day Care!

I want you to know how important you have been to me this year. I have only been able to hold you a few times but every time I do you bring me peace and comfort. I don't know what it is, you have a gift for bringing a sense of calm to the room. This is a gift I hope you always possess. There hasn't been a whole lot of peace and calm in the world this year and we all need it. You remind me of what is right in the world. I thank you for that.

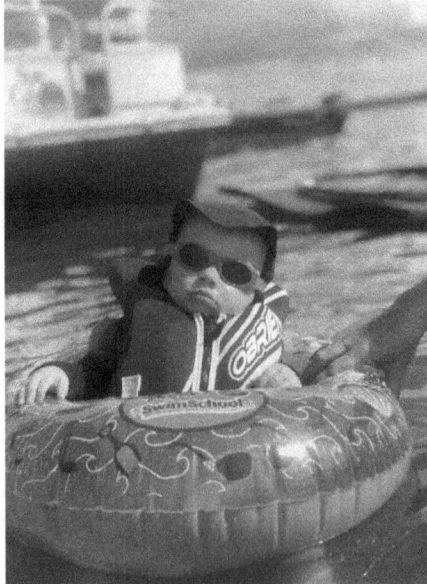

Photo by Alex Turnbull: Hollis, the king of calm.

I hope you are settling into your new house and Day Care. You are only one so that should help you roll with it. I also hope you are establishing your space in your new location. Always respect and treat your sister well but don't be afraid to stand up to her and establish your place in life. She can be a little bossy at times, as you very well know. Pick your battles wisely.

Photo by Alex Turnbull: Mia loves you too!

Grammy and I are looking forward to seeing you at Thanksgiving. I am looking forward to holding you and hanging out for a while. I need your calming effect. Things have been pretty stressful lately. Please don't think it is weird but I will be wearing a mask. I spend every day coaching and working around college kids and it makes me somewhat paranoid.

See you next week! Love you! Love, Grandpa

P.S. That mean orange man you see on television sometimes, will be going away soon. It will be safe to watch the news with your mom and dad again.

ABOUT THE AUTHOR

I am a 61-year-old volleyball coach and success center advisor at Iowa Lakes Community College in Estherville, IA. I ended my retirement after two years to get back into coaching. I just wasn't very good at the retirement thing. I have been here for two years. Aside from all the COVID crap, I love my job. I am not going to complain because I know there are millions who don't have jobs right now. I wouldn't complain anyway, as I already said; I love my job and I am content in knowing I am in the right place at the right time.

I have been blessed throughout my life. My wife and I have been married for thirty-eight + years. We have a beautiful home on Fall Lake outside of Ely, MN. We have two married grown children and three grandchildren. All happy and healthy. My wife runs a successful business in Ely. I spend a large part of the year living and working in Estherville, IA. When I am down here, I live in a Senior apartment on the Good Samaritan Campus. Take note, I said Senior apartment. Not the assisted living or nursing home. If things do take a bad turn though, the Good Sam is a one-stop campus. I could easily be moved to the other facilities.

Think what you want, but I do not know what the end game is, but life is good. I have always said that I might leave coaching feet first someday. That is not the plan, but does anyone really have a plan these days?

Photo by Pam Turnbull: When I turn 62, I would really like to be able to blow out my candles!

JUST SHARING A LITTLE NORMAL

Photo by Alex Turnbull: Great-Great Grandma Toots &
Hollis. He is named after her dad.

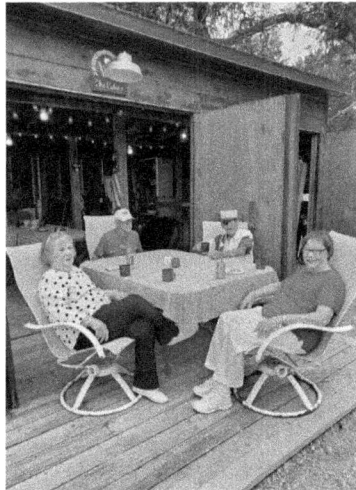

Naomi & Bob LaTourelle/ Rod & Toots Loe

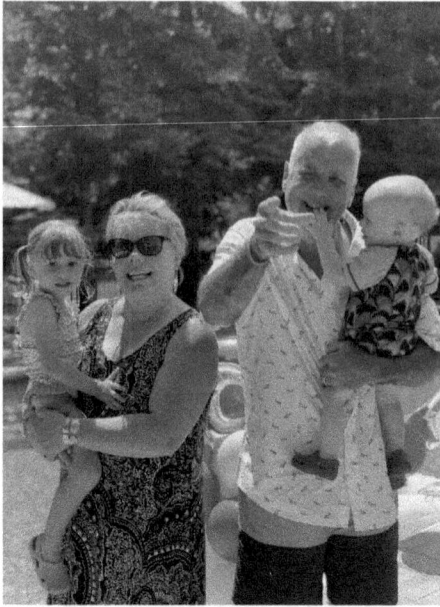

Photo by Alex Turnbull: Brexley, Grammy, Grandpa, & Hollis

Photo by Lexie Baack: Grandpa & Beckett Teaching moment?

Photo by Mike Turnbull

Photo by Mike Turnbull: Fall Lake You should see this in color!

Photo by Mike Turnbull: Annual ride Pam Turnbull, Tootsie, & Mike Loe

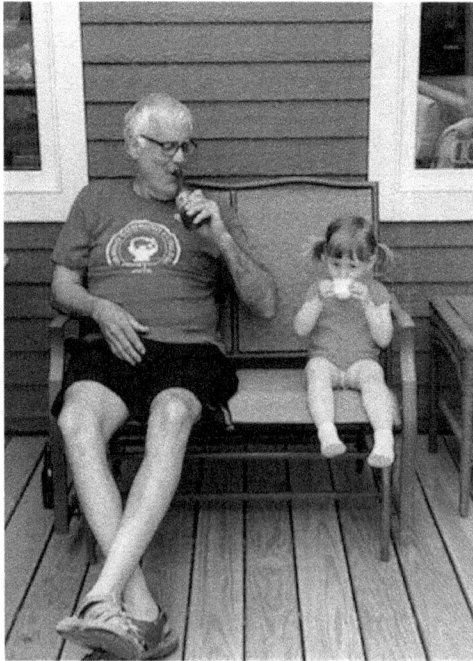

Photo by Alex Turnbull: Tea party on the deck.

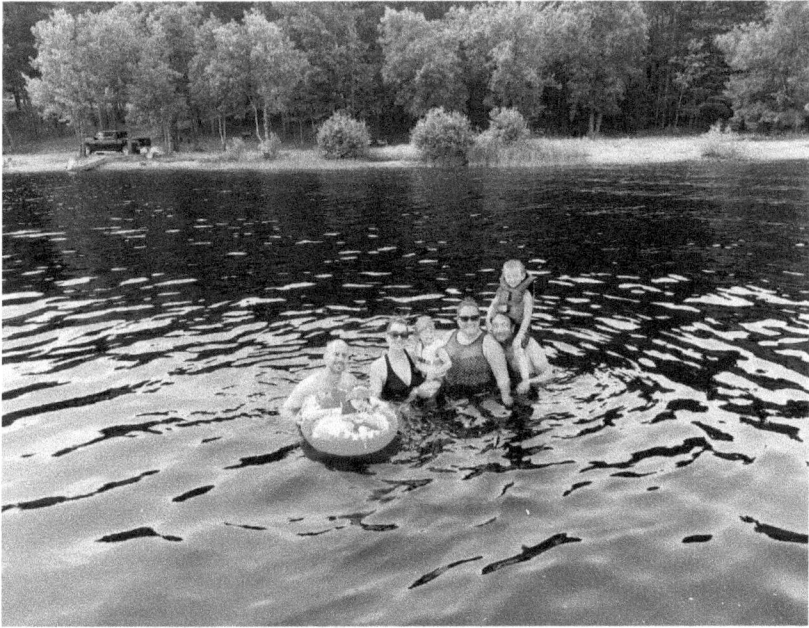

Photo by Mike Turnbull: Summer day on the sandbar;
Hollis, Blaine, Alex, Brexley, Lexie, Beckett & Jeff

Photos by Mike Turnbull
Baacks on the pontoon.

Turnbulls at
Rahja's poolside.

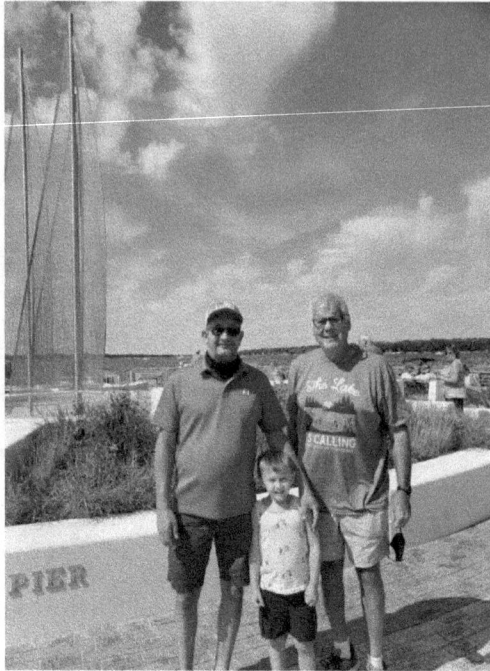

Photo by Lexie Baack: Arnold's Park Pier

Photo by Pam Turnbull: A few years and several hands but the Cabina is done.

Photo by Mike Turnbull: Best opener ever; Nick Petrich cleaned them because he caught most of them & he was taking care of the old guys.

Photo by Patsy Tomlin: Always a proud day when your players graduate. 2020 we graduated five, including Evonne Tomlin. Graduation was in July and she made it back from Texas.

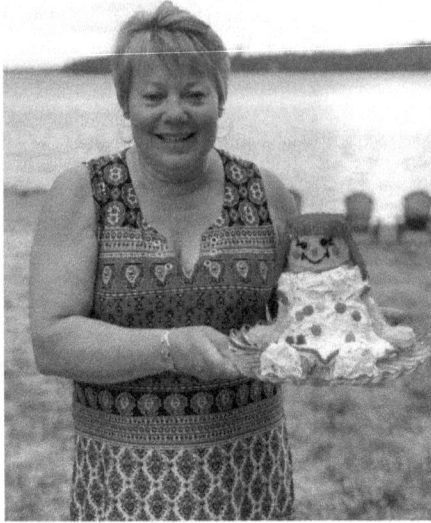

Photo by Alex Turnbull: Pam's 60th Birthday. She made the cake, don't ask!

Photo by Lexie Baack: Hollis is moving up the measuring board.

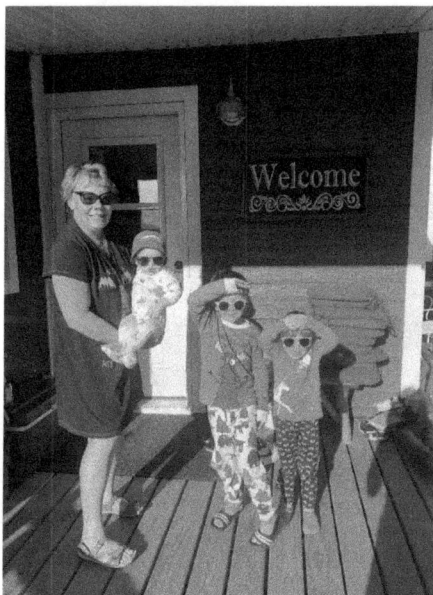

Photo by Alex Turnbull: Good Morning Lake!

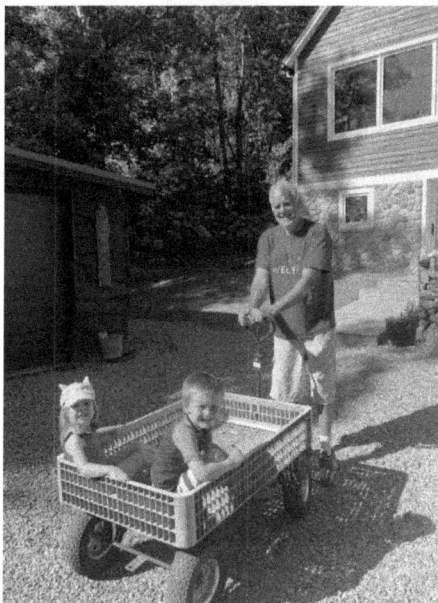

Photo by Pam Turnbull: Off to get more rocks!

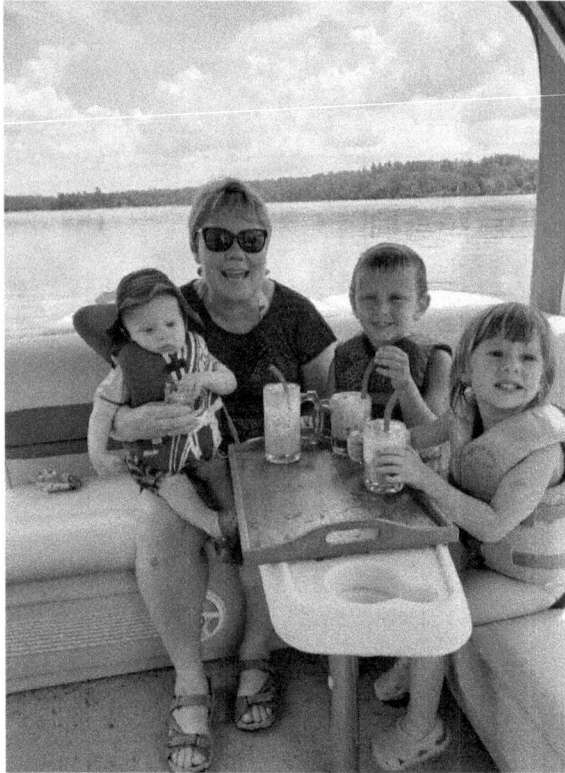

Photo by Alex Turnbull: Fall Lake Floating!

Photo by Evonne Tomlin: Volleyball trip to St. Louis
last fall

Unknown photographer

This is my sister Terri, she works at a nursing home in Austin, MN. She is the strongest person I know. I would have to write an entire book to tell you all the reasons why. I do want you to know that seeing this picture broke my heart but also gave me an over-whelming feeling of pride. I know you can't see it in her eyes but she is a bright, positive, loving, and sym-pathetic person. She cares for and pastors her patients, day in and day out, with no real regard for her wellbe-ing. I can't even comprehend the efforts that she and health care workers across the world have put into this Pandemic. It is obvious that they are all exhausted, but thank God they keep showing up at work. When this is all said and done maybe we should create a Health Care Worker Holiday and annually grant them a one-week paid vacation and celebrate them.

If nothing else, please do everything in your power to protect your health and the health of others and try to take the pressure off these people. They are tapped out!

BOOKS BY MIKE TURNBULL

* All published by Rivershore Books

RANDOM THOUGHTS OF A STUPID MAN

MORE RANDOM THOUGHTS OF A STUPID MAN

STILL A STUPID MAN

A GUIDE TO MIDDLE SCHOOL & BEYOND

I STILL OWN A FLIP PHONE

FIVE DAYS WITHOUT iPADS

RETIREMENT SUCKS!

OBSERVATIONS, QUESTIONS, AND A
FEW ANSWERS

Available in e-books and printed versions.

Available at:

www.rivershorebooks.com
www.amazon.com
www.barnesandnoble.com
www.nookpress.com
www.smashwords.com
Zup's Grocery Store in Ely, MN
Little Swan Lake Winery in Estherville, IA

RIVERSHORE BOOKS

www.rivershorebooks.com
info@rivershorebooks.com
www.facebook.com/rivershore.books
www.twitter.com/rivershorebooks
blog.rivershorebooks.com
forum.rivershorebooks.com